The New

Enchantment of America

INDIANA

By Allan Carpenter

CHILDRENS PRESS, CHICAGO

ACKNOWLEDGMENTS

For assistance in the preparation of the revised edition, the author thanks:
SIMONE H. SMILJANIC, Advertising Specialist, and TAMARA L. SCHORNSTEIN, Photography Librarian, Department of Commerce, State of Indiana.

American Airlines—Anne Vitaliano, Director of Public Relations; *Capitol Historical Society*, Washington, D. C.; *Newberry Library,* Chicago, Dr. Lawrence Towner, Director; *Northwestern University Library*, Evanston, Illinois; *United Airlines*—John P. Grember, Manager of Special Promotions; Joseph P. Hopkins, Manager, News Bureau.

UNITED STATES GOVERNMENT AGENCIES: *Department of Agriculture*—Robert Hailstock, Jr., Photography Division, Office of Communication; Donald C. Schuhart, Information Division, Soil Conservation Service. *Army*—Doran Topolosky, Public Affairs Office, Chief of Engineers, Corps of Engineers. *Department of Interior*—Louis Churchville, Director of Communications; EROS Space Program—Phillis Wiepking, Community Affairs; Charles Withington, Geologist; Mrs. Ruth Herbert, Information Specialist; Bureau of Reclamation; National Park Service—Fred Bell and the individual sites; Fish and Wildlife Service—Bob Hines, Public Affairs Office. *Library of Congress*—Dr. Alan Fern, Director of the Department of Research; Sara Wallace, Director of Publications; Dr. Walter W. Ristow, Chief, Geography and Map Division; Herbert Sandborn, Exhibits Officer. *National Archives*—Dr. James B. Rhoads, Archivist of the United States; Albert Meisel, Assistant Archivist for Educational Programs; David Eggenberger, Publications Director; Bill Leary, Still Picture Reference; James Moore, Audio-Visual Archives. *United States Postal Service*—Herb Harris, Stamps Division.

For assistance in the preparation of the first edition, the author thanks:
Robert McClarren, Director, Indiana State Library; Matthew Empson Welsh, former governor; Mabel D. Stanfield; Warren A. Reeder, Jr.; Roger D. Branigin; State Historical Bureau; State Department of Commerce and Public Relations.

Illustrations on the preceding pages:
Cover photograph: Indiana Dunes at sunset, Jim Rowan
Page 1: Commemorative stamps of historic interest
Pages 2-3: Covered Bridge, Parke County, Richard Cunningham
Page 3 (Map): USDI Geological Survey
Pages 4-5: Indianapolis area, EROS Space Photo, USDI Geological Survey, EROS Data Center

Project Editor, Revised Edition:
 Joan Downing
Assistant Editor, Revised Edition:
 Mary Reidy

Library of Congress Cataloging in Publication Data

Carpenter, John Allan, 1917-
 Indiana.

 (His The new enchantment of America)
 SUMMARY: The Hoosier State, including its history from earliest times to the present, its famous citizens, and places of interest.
 1. Indiana—Juvenile literature.
[1. Indiana] I. Title. II. Series: Carpenter, John Allan, 1917- The new enchantment of America.
F526.3.C3 1979 977.2 78-12459
ISBN 0-516-04114-2

Contents

"JOHNNY
APPLESEED"
JOHN CHAPMAN
HE LIVED FOR OTHERS
HOLY BIBLE
1774 1845

A True Story to Set the Scene

On a warm summer day in 1845, a strange-looking figure approached the home of a settler in Allen County, Indiana. He was dressed in a coffee-sack shirt and wore a pasteboard hat with a peak to keep off the sun. There were no shoes on his aged and leathery feet. The visitor was warmly greeted by the settler and his family, as he always had been by thousands of other pioneers across a vast territory.

The visitor refused to eat with the family, but accepted some bread and milk to eat on the front porch. After he had preached on the Beatitudes, the family retired and the visitor lay down, as he was accustomed to do, on the bare floor. In the morning the visitor was dead. Thus ended the life of one of the memorable men of pioneer times whose life, especially in later years, is part of the enchantment of Indiana.

This was John (or Jonathan) Chapman. He often told of being kicked by a horse when he was twenty-six years old and of then having a vision of heaven. The heaven he saw in his vision was filled with endless rows of apple trees in full bloom. John Chapman devoted the rest of his life to making that dream come true on earth, feeling that working to produce such fruit was the closest thing to true religion.

In countless trips to the cider presses of Pennsylvania, he obtained innumerable apple seeds, which he stuffed into leather bags and carried into the wilderness area of the Ohio River Valley. As Ohio became populated, he moved into Indiana. Wherever he found a suitable spot, he planted his precious seeds, seeming always to remember where they had been planted throughout the huge area of his travels. Occasionally he returned to cultivate the thriving trees. He became known far and wide as Johnny Appleseed.

Barefooted, Johnny tramped across the wilderness, impervious to stones, thorns, and even rattlesnakes. If someone gave him a pair of

Opposite: Johnny Appleseed's grave, Fort Wayne.

shoes, he usually passed them on immediately to a poor family. He called his coffee-sack shirt a "very serviceable cloak."

The Indians respected him as a great medicine man and treated him with remarkable kindness. Wherever he went, he was greatly loved, especially by children.

Johnny Appleseed practiced the "reverence for life" for which Dr. Albert Schweitzer became famous so many years later. Johnny could not bear to harm a living thing. When mosquitoes flew into his campfire, he would put the fire out to save them from burning. Once, when a rattlesnake bit him, he killed it, and never overcame his regret for the act. Whenever he saw a domestic animal abused, he would buy it and give it to someone he was sure would treat it well.

He preached the religion of Emanuel Swedenborg and often gave fiery sermons to his pioneer listeners. The memorable scene of Johnny Appleseed preaching in the wilderness, dressed in his strange clothes, stayed with most of those who heard him until the day they died.

He devoted the last forty-six of his seventy-one years of life to his self-imposed tasks of planting and preaching.

His work literally "bore fruit" over 100,000 square miles (260,000 square kilometers). He had an uncanny knack of selecting favorable sites for his orchards, but many are now the locations of thriving cities. In many other places, his orchards still open their blossoms to the spring air and bear fruit, living memorials to a man who "reached with one hand downward to the lowest forms of life, and with the other upward to the very throne of God."

His sturdy individualism, imagination, and spiritual qualities have been especially typical of the people of Indiana over the years.

Lay of the Land

"I shall never forget the thrill with which as a boy I first learned that Fort Wayne was connected directly by water with the Atlantic Ocean! The St. Marys and St. Joe rivers joined in Fort Wayne to form the Maumee; this flowed directly into Lake Erie, and by the Niagara River, Lake Ontario, and the St. Lawrence there was direct connection by water between Fort Wayne and the mighty ocean. . . . With good luck a chip thrown into the water a few blocks from my home would reach the Atlantic."

A lesson in geography had "come alive" for one Indiana boy, and it can come alive for all who examine the wandering rivers, sparkling lakes, sandy "conservatories," fertile plains, and picturesque hills of the state.

THE LAND TODAY

Like the Maumee, some Indiana rivers flow to the Atlantic through the St. Lawrence River system. Others reach the same ocean by way of the Mississippi system. The slope which divides these two great river systems is so gradual as it runs through Indiana that it is hardly apparent to the eye. Many small tributary streams have their beginnings only a few feet apart and yet some empty into the Gulf of St. Lawrence and others into the Gulf of Mexico.

If the boy who wanted to float a chip to the ocean had looked at the map more closely, he would have found another interesting fact about the three Indiana rivers he mentioned. The St. Joseph flows south and west; the St. Marys flows north and west. When they come together they form the Maumee, which suddenly flows almost directly to the east, a rare situation among rivers.

Two major rivers are especially associated with Indiana—the mighty Ohio and the storied Wabash. The Ohio serves as the entire southern boundary of Indiana; the Wabash has an unusual course, flowing northwest, then west, then southwest, and finally south, to make a meandering border between Illinois and Indiana.

The Wabash and the Ohio are the only Indiana rivers that are on the U.S. Geological Survey's list of principal rivers of the United States.

Other prominent Indiana rivers include the second of two that are named St. Joseph, that is, the one that flows through South Bend; the Whitewater; Kankakee; Iroquois; Tippecanoe; Eel; White; Patoka; Blue; Big Blue; Mississinewa; and Salamonie. The elusive Lost River (in Washington, Orange, Martin counties) flows on the surface and then flows underground, to reappear and disappear at intervals, depending in some places on the amount of rainfall. Twenty-two miles (35.4 kilometers) of its course are underground.

There are almost thirteen hundred lakes in Indiana—most of them in the northeastern section. Lake Wawasee, southeast of Goshen, is the largest natural lake in the state, with Lake Maxinkuckee second,

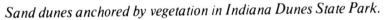

Sand dunes anchored by vegetation in Indiana Dunes State Park.

and Lake James third. Monroe Reservoir is the largest body of water within the state.

Indiana's 51-mile (82-kilometer) strip of Lake Michigan coast provides an invaluable toehold for the state on the Great Lakes, and 25 miles (40.2 kilometers) of that lakeshore are dominated by the Indiana Dunes, a region which in some respects is unlike any other in the world.

These magnificent dunes are formed by many interesting forces. The motion of the water crushes rock to sand, which is brought to shore by waves. Winds, which generally come from the north or northwest, pick up the sand and carry it inland, dumping it in huge piles. Vines, shrubs, or trees may grow in the sand, helping to anchor it. Then more sand is blown in and caught, and finally a dune forms. "Live" dunes are those that are not anchored by vegetation, and they move across the region as the winds shift the sand. Whole areas may be covered or uncovered as the sand shifts.

In general, the present-day surface of Indiana is divided into three main regions: the northern lake country, the central agricultural plain, and the southern hills and lowlands.

CLIMATE

Winters in Indiana are relatively mild, particularly in the southern part of the state. Summers are likely to be hot and humid, with a good deal of rainfall. Average precipitation for the state is 40 inches (101.6 centimeters). Only a small percentage of this moisture comes in the form of snow. However, the Lake Michigan region is noted for occasional storms that pile up enormous amounts of snow, which has been gathered in the long sweep down the great lake.

THE LAND AS IT WAS

At least five-sixths of what is now Indiana was buried, at one time or other, under the crushing weight of glaciers. Only the small south-

Indiana Dunes National Lakeshore.

central "driftless" area completely escaped the glaciers. These covers of ice, coming at least three different times, were the principal forces that shaped the land as we know it today.

The glaciers leveled hills, filled in valleys, and piled up hills and cliffs called moraines. They dug out holes and low areas which later filled to become lakes and swamps. They filled part of the bed of the Ohio River with debris and leveled the central portion of the state by filling it in with vast quantities of rock, sand, and fine soil, scooped out and dragged down from farther north.

Many millions of years before the glaciers, the area now called Indiana was covered by seas. They came and receded over eons of time. Great upheavals raised or lowered portions of the earth.

As time went on, plants and animals flourished in the region. They, too, came and went, covered again by the ancient seas. Sometimes hardened bones of the giant mammoth and mastodon are found in the northern part of the state.

Footsteps on the Land

THE ANCIENT ONES

The relics they left behind tell us all we know about "prehistoric" people—those who lived in a region before records were kept. Archaeologists study these remains and try to learn what the prehistoric people must have been like. Indiana is rich in archaeological treasures.

A large part of these treasures is found in the mounds built by the ancient peoples. These mounds were used as elevated sites for houses or temples, fortifications, or burial places. Some were simply formed by the dumping of refuse over the years.

Some of the most interesting Indiana mounds are in Mounds State Park, where an amusement park merry-go-round placed on a rare "fiddle-back" mound almost destroyed it—before the area was preserved by the state government.

The different people and different periods of ancient times have been given various names. Those in Indiana include the so-called Adena, Fort Ancient, and Hopewell cultures.

Ancient people in Indiana were studied intensively by J. Arthur MacLean in 1926 and 1927. He studied their work in polished stone, basketry, textiles, and even copper, and found that they used the bow and arrow and had domesticated animals.

Nothing is known of what became of these people—whether they were killed, died, or went away. It is possible that the Indians of a later date were descendants of one or more of the ancient peoples, but this has never been established.

THE "BRONZE-SKINNED ONES"

The land that is now Indiana must have been a little eerie during the period when white men were first settling on the east coast of North America. All evidence indicates that the present area of Indiana was almost uninhabited at that time. The reason is not known, but it is thought that if there had previously been Indian dwellers there, they had fled because of invasions of fierce Iroquois Indians from the east.

Only a short time before Europeans came into the land we now call Indiana, Indians began to settle there. When white men arrived, they found the Miami and Potawatomi to be the most important people in the region. Others were the Wea, Kickapoo, Piankashaw, Chippewa, Illinois, Ottawa, Wyandot, and Shawnee. Some of the groups had been driven from their ancestral lands in the east by European settlement. These included the Delaware Indians, who obtained permission to enter the region as late as 1770.

The Miami had a relatively high organization. Each tribe was led by four chiefs: a man and a woman war chief, and a man and a woman civil chief. These positions were inherited through the father. On the night before battle, each warrior brought his good-luck "medicine" to the council house, and all of these charms were wrapped in a bundle which the medicine man carried into the conflict. After a victory the bundle was opened, and each man claimed his "medicine" amid ceremonies and festivities.

There were many great Indian leaders in Indiana, and the Indians dominated the region for many years. Almost no trace of their influence remains today, however, except for museum exhibits and the names they left for various places: Muncie, Mishawaka, Miami, Winona, Wawasee, Kokomo, Kankakee, Maxinkukee, Mississinewa, and Maumee. Most prominent in Indiana is a word from the long-forgotten language of the Miami: *Wa-pe-sha,* the well-loved "Wabash" of today. Of course, the very name of the state, Indiana, is a continual reminder of the Indian heritage.

THE "LIGHT-SKINNED ONES"

Did a strange group of "white" Indians live in Indiana as early as the year 1200? Most authorities think this is only legend. However, it makes an interesting story.

16

War Dance of the Winnebago, *by Peter Rindisbacher.*

Madoc, son of the Prince of Wales, is reported to have sailed "into the west" from Wales to seek his fortune. Some writers claimed that he and his party made their way to the Falls of the Ohio, and occupied a natural fortification at Rose Island. Indians told travelers of a "strange race" that once lived there. Legends also persist that some Welsh words have been found in the Indian languages, that a piece of Welsh armor was found on the banks of the Ohio River, and that early hunters stumbled over a tombstone dated 1186. These stories are not taken seriously at the present time.

Historian Dr. Charles Slocum says that Samuel de Champlain reached the site of what is now Fort Wayne in 1614, but European exploration of the area now called Indiana was not recorded in generally accepted accounts until much later. Possibly, explorers and Jesuit priests touched the Michigan shore in the early days of French settlement along the St. Lawrence, but no reliable records have been found of this. Probably Father Jacques Marquette passed through

17

the region of Gary in 1673, but this is not certainly known. Some historians believe that Father Claude Allouez passed through in about the same period.

The earliest record of European exploration in Indiana is that of Robert Cavalier, Sieur de La Salle. In late 1679, he and his party entered the mouth of the St. Joseph River near present-day Benton Harbor, Michigan, and pushed up the river, reaching its most southerly bend, where South Bend now stands, on December 3. Next day they carried their boats and supplies over the portage to the Kankakee River and sailed into what is now Illinois, the first Europeans known to enter and cross Indiana.

Two years later, La Salle called together a grand council of the Indians beneath the spreading branches of a great tree which came to be called Council Oak, in present-day South Bend. They agreed on many points concerning trade and the establishment of strongpoints. La Salle recommended that the French build a string of forts across Indiana and Illinois to protect their interests in North America. He was killed in 1687 on a colonizing expedition in Texas before his plan could be carried out.

Later, however, the forts were built. There is great uncertainty about exact dates. Some assert that the first fort, Fort of the Miamis, where Fort Wayne now stands, was built as early as 1700 at the Indian town of Kekionga. Others say it was built in 1714. Near Lafayette, Fort Ouiatenon was built sometime between 1717 and 1719, depending on whose dates you accept. On the lower Wabash River, François Morgane de Vincennes established the fort that bears his name, probably in the period 1727-1732. However, some sources say that there may have been a French fort at Vincennes as early as 1708. Soon after the fort was established by Vincennes, a number of French families settled around Fort Vincennes, making this the first permanent European settlement in what is now Indiana.

These three forts protected the travel route between the two great French provinces of North America—Louisiana and Canada. Forts Miami and Ouiatenon were part of the huge province of Canada, and Vincennes was in the even larger province of Louisiana. The route between the two provinces was long and difficult. From Lake Erie, the French travelers paddled up the Maumee River to the portage at Fort Miami. Crossing the portage, they launched their canoes in the Little Wabash and had an uninterrupted water passage over the vast wilderness to New Orleans by way of the Little Wabash, the Ohio, and finally the great Mississippi. There were other routes—over the St. Joseph and Kankakee rivers portage or over the Chicago and Des Plaines rivers portage—but the Maumee-Little Wabash portage was called "the Glorious Gate" because of the comparatively easy passage it gave and its importance in the communications of French North America.

In these huge wilderness areas, fur trading was the most important commercial activity. Licensed traders, called *voyageurs,* brought ammunition, blankets, hatchets, utensils, ornaments, beads, and brandy to exchange with the Indians for furs of great value.

The French settlers in Indiana were a good-natured group. They loved to dance and play games. They accepted the Indians, treating

The Voyageurs, *painting by Charles Deas.*

them as equals. Frenchmen often married Indian women and they lived together happily. The Catholic church was the most important center of life at Vincennes.

All over the world there was great rivalry between the British and French for control of the rich and undeveloped regions of the globe. Toward the middle of the 1700s, British traders became more and more successful in the French regions, including Indiana. The French sent a peculiar but colorful expedition, under the leadership of Jean Baptiste Celoron de Bienville, down the Ohio Valley to reassert France's claim to the area, to warn British traders away, and to increase the friendship of the Indians.

At Fort Miami, the story is told, Celoron found a friendly chief with an interesting name — *le Pied Froid,* which means "Cold Foot" in French. One writer says, "I have frittered away considerable time in wondering whether he was so called because of poor circulatory system or native timidity." However, this is probably a legend, as there is doubt that Celoron visited Fort Miami.

In North America, French-British rivalry eventually turned into what was called the French and Indian War. By 1763 the French had been forced to give up all their holdings on the North American continent, and British troops occupied the two northern French forts in Indiana.

REBELLIONS AND REVOLUTIONS

In order to preserve the wilderness for the fur trade, the British king issued his Proclamation of 1763. This prohibited settlement "beyond the heads of the Atlantic rivers." Only licensed traders were to enter the area. This order kept out all but a few outlaws and squatters.

The British did not bring civil law into the region, and the French settlers and traders who remained there had to get along with local customs and regulations.

At first the British and Indians did not get along well together, because the British treated the Indians in a high-handed, arrogant manner, entirely differently than the French treated them. The great Chief Pontiac organized many Indian groups into a strong confederacy to drive the English from their western lands. Lieutenant Jenkins and his force at Fort Ouiatenon were compelled to surrender in Pontiac's so-called conspiracy.

As one writer says, "That name 'conspiracy' is as improper as any we arrogant whites ever fastened upon an event in history. Far from the dishonorable shadow the term implies, Pontiac's was a legitimate defensive action designed to save his people's lands and their culture."

A local historian describes the events when Pontiac's forces attacked Fort Miami. The commander, Ensign Holmes, "was lured from the security of the fort by a false plea of his Indian sweetheart and was shot down by Indians secreted in the near-by shrubbery." All British forces were swept out of what is now Indiana, but the attack on Detroit failed, and eventually Pontiac was unsuccessful.

No British troops again occupied Indiana until 1777, when Henry Hamilton, British commander at Detroit, sent soldiers to Vincennes. By this time the revolution of the American colonies against Britain was in full swing. Most of the Indians in Indiana chose to take sides with the British. They realized that if the Americans won the war, they would settle on Indian lands and drive the Indians away.

Hamilton encouraged the Indians to take American scalps and was given the nickname "Hair Buyer." The year 1777 has long been known as the "bloody year" because of fierce Indian attacks.

Much of the history of the Revolutionary War in what was then "the west" deals with the brilliant work of a young Kentucky officer, George Rogers Clark. Through her original charter of 1609, Virginia claimed what is now Kentucky, Illinois, and Indiana. Clark persuaded Governor Patrick Henry of Virginia that the American colonies would never be safe if the British continued to control the territories at the colonies' back door. So Virginia gave support to Clark's plan to drive the British from the west.

With only a handful of men, Clark captured Kaskaskia, Illinois, without a struggle and won the French residents to his side. Father Gibault, a beloved priest, agreed to hurry to Vincennes and he persuaded the French there to take an oath to support America. There was no English garrison at Vincennes at that moment.

Enraged at this news, "Hair Buyer" Hamilton himself marched on Vincennes from Detroit with an army of six hundred and recaptured it in December of 1778. Hamilton was sure Clark could not attack until spring; so he kept only a small force of men and dismissed the rest of his soldiers for the winter.

One of the rich traders of Vincennes, courageous Francis Vigo, made the dangerous escape from Vincennes and began a journey full of hardship to bring this news to Clark at Kaskaskia. Without Vigo's journey, Clark might never have learned how the garrison at Vincennes had been weakened.

Clark expected that in the spring Hamilton would gather a large army again and might easily drive the American forces out of the west forever. Yet it seemed impossible for any force to march across the 240 miles (676 kilometers) from Kaskaskia to Vincennes during the winter. Clark wrote to Governor Henry, "I know the case is desperate, but, Sir, we must either quit the country or attack Mr. Hamilton. No time is to be lost. Was I sure of a re-enforcement I should not attempt it. Who knows what fortune will do for us? Great things have been effected by a few men well conducted. Perhaps we may be fortunate."

He was right. He and his men were soon to perform one of the "great things" of American history.

On February 5, Clark marched from Kaskaskia at the head of about 170 troops. There had been a great deal of chilly rain, and most of the lowlands were flooded. This meant the men had long stretches of wading through icy water, with little opportunity to dry their clothes at campfires. Sometimes they could barely keep their rifles and ammunition dry.

A drummer boy helped to maintain their morale with his antics, such as floating across a flooded marsh on his drum, but there was little else to be cheerful about. Approaching Vincennes, the troops could not light fires to dry their clothes and had to stay soaked. Their supply boat failed to keep up with them, and they went the last two days without food.

Surrender of Colonel Henry Hamilton to George Rogers Clark at Ft. Sackville, *an Ezra Winter mural.*

Reaching Vincennes, Clark spread his men as far apart as possible. The women of Kaskaskia had made twenty American flags, and these, too, were spaced well apart. As the men advanced in the dusk, they zig-zagged back and forth to give the effect of greater numbers. Suddenly the startled British defenders found themselves facing an invading force of what appeared to be a great army of "twenty companies."

Creeping so near to the fort that the cannons could not touch them, Clark and his men fired whenever they spotted a light through the portholes, but their ammunition was running low. At the critical moment some of the French people of Vincennes escaped and showed the Americans where they had hidden a supply of ammunition. This maintained the American firing.

When day came, a group of Indians arrived at the fort, bringing scalps of American settlers in Kentucky to claim their reward from "Hair Buyer" Hamilton. Clark had four of these Indians shot in full view of the fort as a warning to other Indians. At last, Hamilton surrendered and became a captive. This was one of the most important engagements by Americans during the Revolution. Clark's victory has been called "one of the greatest exploits of American arms."

Although Clark was never able to marshal the forces to make his dream of taking Detroit come true, he made a great contribution to his new country. Without his successes in the old Northwest region, America would have had little claim on the area from which came Ohio, Illinois, Michigan, Wisconsin, parts of Minnesota, and of course Indiana. Except for the imagination and daring of one man, George Rogers Clark, all of that vast area might now be part of Canada.

THIS ONCE WAS THE "WILD WEST"

The Revolutionary War ended with the Treaty of Paris, and the Northwest Territory was turned over to the new United States. From near Canada to Florida, the Mississippi became the western boundary. However, the country had a very shaky hold on its western frontier. England simply ignored her promise to get out of the Northwest and maintained her hold at Detroit and other places. The British and Indians were in actual control of much of the Northwest.

Not even the English were entirely safe from the Indians. There is an interesting story of the capture of a young Englishman, Thomas Ridout, by the Shawnee. A Shawnee leader named Kakinathucca took a liking to him and decided to take Ridout personally to Detroit, where his friends could ransom him. Ridout has a fascinating account of Indian life in the Indiana woods. Kakinathucca's wife "cut some venison . . . into small pieces and seasoning it with dry herbs she put the whole into a frying pan with bear's oil; she also boiled some water in a copper kettle, with which she made tea in a teapot, using cups and saucers of yellow ware . . . she poured some tea in a saucer, which, with some fried meat on a pewter plate she gave me. This was a luxury I little expected to meet with. . . . The tea proved to be green tea and was sweetened with maple sugar." They finally reached Fort Wayne and eventually Detroit, where Ridout regained his freedom.

In spite of Indian dangers, however, Americans were anxious to settle in the new territories. Virginia gave George Rogers Clark and

24

his men a grant of 150,000 acres (60,700 hectares) for their services, and in 1783 or 1784 Clark established and laid out the town of Clarksville, Indiana—the first authorized American settlement in the Northwest Territory.

Virginia and other eastern states gave up their claims to western lands, and in 1787 Congress passed an "ordinance for the government of the territory northwest of the River Ohio"—the famous Northwest Ordinance, one of the most important laws in American history. During that same year, Major John F. Hamtramck took command at Vincennes. In 1790, Acting Governor Winthrop Sargent set up local government there.

The Indians were alarmed. The lands were theirs. The prospect of more and more settlers taking over their lands made the Miami form a confederacy under Chief Little Turtle, and they went on the war-path, encouraged by the British. General Josiah Harmer was defeated by Little Turtle in a battle within the boundaries of present-day Fort Wayne. General Arthur St. Clair, governor of the North-west Territory, was also defeated by Little Turtle's forces, in a battle just over the border in Ohio, near the headwaters of the Wabash.

Disturbed by the Indian victories, President George Washington sent an unusual man to the Northwest—General Anthony Wayne. He had been so fearless in the Revolutionary War he was known as "Mad" Anthony Wayne. He trained his forces in all the practices of Indian warfare and finally marched northward, at the same time encouraging the Indians to settle their troubles peacefully.

Chief Little Turtle recognized the growing American strength. He urged his fellow chiefs in the Miami Confederacy to make a treaty with the new government. But they called him a coward and took away much of his authority.

On the banks of the Maumee, in a woodland where many trees had been blown over in the wind, General Wayne defeated the Indians in the Battle of Fallen Timbers in Ohio, not far from the Indiana border. As a sidelight, it can be pointed out that General Wayne's assistant could be called Whistler's father-in-law. He was the father of the wife of the painter who made his mother famous with her portrait.

A painting of the Battle of Fallen Timbers, 1794, when General "Mad" Anthony Wayne and his forces defeated the Indians.

After the victory of Fallen Timbers, General Wayne built the fort that bears his name on the site of old Fort Miami, and this was the beginning of Fort Wayne. He forced the Indian leaders to attend a great meeting at Green Ville, Ohio. After months of "palaver" they signed the Treaty of Green Ville. Among many other provisions, this treaty opened southeastern Indiana (the Whitewater Valley region) to American settlement. The Indiana region enjoyed comparative peace for about fifteen years.

INDIANA TERRITORY

In 1800 Congress split the Northwest Territory and created the Indiana Territory. This included the present states of Illinois, Wisconsin, Michigan, and part of Minnesota, as well as Indiana. President John Adams named William Henry Harrison as first governor of this new territory.

Governor Harrison arrived at Vincennes in 1801 to set up a "rude makeshift" government. His major problem was opening the land. Settlers were pressing for the right to get title to lands in Indiana Territory, yet most of the land technically belonged to the Indians. One of Governor Harrison's greatest accomplishments was to obtain, by 1809, rights to almost the entire southern third of present-day Indiana, through peaceful negotiations with the Indians.

During this period, Michigan was separated from the Indiana Territory. The first General Assembly of the Indiana Territory met in 1805 at Vincennes, and in 1809 the Indiana Territory was reduced to the present area of the state.

One of the strangest episodes in American history took place in part in Indiana: the events revolving around Aaron Burr, former vice president of the United States. Burr met Major Davis Floyd in Jeffersonville and interested him in a plan to conquer Mexico. Floyd was hoodwinked into thinking that this was a secret plan of the United States government which Burr was carrying out.

Because Mexico was controlled by Spain and Spain was at peace with the United States, Floyd recruited men by telling them they would be colonists. He also built a fleet of boats near present-day New Albany. Burr's real designs have never been known, but it is generally thought he planned to form an empire of his own west of the Mississippi.

Floyd was arrested for his part in the undertaking and convicted of treason. Many thought he was a real traitor, while others felt he was loyal but deceived. He was fined $20 and given a three-hour jail sentence. In 1807, Burr was tried for treason but was found not guilty.

MORE BATTLES

Encouraged by the British, the Indians became more difficult. They were led by two remarkable Indian men: the strange but powerful figure known as the Prophet and his half-brother, the great Chief Tecumseh. Meeting with Governor Harrison in 1810 and 1811, Tecumseh denounced the Indians' practice of making land grants to the white men. He decided to gather all western tribes into a great confederacy to oppose further white advances.

They set up their headquarters, called Prophetstown, near the present city of Lafayette. In the fall of 1811, Governor Harrison assembled an army of about a thousand men and marched north. He established Fort Harrison near Terre Haute, then marched along the Tippecanoe River until he was close to Prophetstown, on November 7,

1811. Tecumseh was away in the south at the time, trying to get more tribes to join his confederacy.

The Prophet sent word that he would like a council with Harrison the next day, but he treacherously attacked before the council was scheduled. However, Harrison was on guard, and a battle occurred, with heavy losses on both sides. The importance of this Battle of Tippecanoe at Prophetstown was later much exaggerated, although it set back the Indian cause; the Prophet lost face and Prophetstown was destroyed. It was learned later that Tecumseh was greatly distressed because his brother had gone into battle.

When the War of 1812 came, many Indians fought with the British, and Tecumseh was made an officer in the British army. Forts Harrison and Wayne were besieged but managed to hold out. At Pigeon Roost in southern Indiana, near present Scottsburg, the Indians massacred twenty whites (mostly women and children), and settlers were harassed all through the war. Only a few Miami, under Little Turtle, took no part in the war.

General Harrison resigned as governor of Indiana to become a wartime commander. One of his great successes during the war was the Battle of the Thames in Canada, when he defeated British General Proctor and Tecumseh, and the mighty chief was killed.

A SOVEREIGN STATE

By the end of the war, Indiana was largely free from fear of Indian attack. In 1813 the capital was moved from Vincennes to Corydon, and the population had grown to about thirty thousand. By 1816 it had more than doubled, to beyond sixty thousand. People were coming from the East and from Europe to start new lives. Among them were Thomas Lincoln and his family from Kentucky, of whom much more would be heard.

Indiana was ready for a whole new life, and on December 11, 1816, it became the nineteenth state of the United States. Jonathan Jennings was its first governor, and James Noble and Waller Taylor its first United States senators.

Yesterday and Today

PIONEER LIFE IN INDIANA

"We lived the same as Indians 'ceptin' we took an interest in politics and religion." This was the way Dennis Hanks, cousin of Abraham Lincoln, described pioneer life in Indiana a year after statehood. Lincoln himself wrote of his boyhood home near present Buffaloville as "a wild region with bears and other wild animals still in the woods. The clearing away of surplus wood was the great task ahead." The pioneers had difficult times with the overwhelming stands of trees in the "ceaseless" forests.

Another pioneer recalled, "We children slept in crude lofts over the main room of the cabin. The lofts were reached by peg 'ladders' driven into the log walls. Many a winter morning I remember waking as the fine snow filtered through the cracks above, caressing my face and drifting over the coverlet."

This was luxury, however, compared to the first homes made by those just arriving in the wilderness. To get some kind of shelter, the first task of a new family was to build a "half-faced" camp. Two Y-shaped poles held a cross pole about 12 feet (3.7 meters) from a large fallen tree. Lighter poles were laid slantingly from the cross pole to the fallen tree, to make a roof. Thick brush was piled up for a kind of shingling, and small poles were laid on top of one another to cover the sides. The front was open, and a fire was kept burning there for heating and cooking.

Half-faced camps were all right for the summer months, but a family had to build a sturdy, tight log cabin for winter. All the pioneer families for miles around would gather to help. A "house raising" was one of the few social gatherings of the early settlers. When the work was over, everyone would eat a hearty meal, prepared by the women. There were songs, dancing, races, and games. When fields had to be cleared of trees, log-rolling "parties" were held, and again all the neighbors helped and had a good time.

An iron skillet was the only cooking utensil owned by many pioneer mothers. The woman who also owned an iron pot kettle was considered an "aristocrat." Those who were fortunate might have brought with them some bedding, a spinning wheel, clock, and chest of drawers. Because manufactured items were so costly to ship into the wilderness, most pioneer families made almost everything they needed—clothing of skins or homespun cloth, soap, candles, crude furniture.

A bed would be made by setting a post in the floor, with bed rails reaching both ways to the cabin walls. Rope wound back and forth became a bedspring, and the mattress was a cloth bag stuffed with wild grass or straw. Benches and stools were made of slabs of logs.

Pioneer families of ten or twelve children were common, and they enjoyed playthings made from the simple materials at hand. Baby played with a rattle made of a gourd, with its seeds dried. Corn husks

A restored pioneer village at Spring Mill State Park in Mitchell shows how the pioneers of the early 1800s lived in Indiana.

were fashioned into dolls with corn-silk hair. Sharp jackknives carved many a top and willow whistle. The forerunners of present-day baseballs were fashioned by wrapping stones with yarn and covering the whole with deerskin.

Girls made necklaces by stringing berries or seeds. They learned to sew or knit when they could first hold the needles. Many children found live "playthings" in the woods and tamed 'possums, raccoons, squirrels, crows, or even bear cubs and fawns.

On winter evenings, apples might be roasted and corn popped over the hearth fire; while old and young went about their tasks, they might sing hymns, or ballads, or recite Bible passages.

Many a pioneer Indiana boy was taught the lore of the woods—hunting, trapping, fishing—by an Indian friend.

The Sheek House at Spring Mill State Park was built in 1816.

One of the prize pioneer crafts was the making of coverlets. These were of wool clipped from local sheep, washed, spun, dyed, and woven by the women. The designs were first made on a sort of blueprint on paper. The most desired were often exchanged, just as recipes might be. Some of the best coverlets may be seen in museums. Many of these are very beautiful.

As pioneer communities advanced, they could afford the work of saddlers, harness makers, shoemakers, tinsmiths, plasterers, carpenters, brick masons, wireworkers, tailors, and even hatters. These were men (and sometimes women) of great skill who usually had fierce pride in the quality of their handiwork.

A YOUNG STATE GROWS

In 1818 the Delaware Indians agreed by treaty to give up their claims to most of the central part of the state, in what was called the "New Purchase," and they promised to leave for the west within three years of the purchase.

Corydon, which had been the territorial capital from 1813 to 1816 and state capital thereafter, was not suitable because of its location. A commission of ten members studied many proposed locations, and in 1820 decided on a rolling woodland site in a region of few Indian villages and only two white settlers—the future Indianapolis.

In the same year, Indiana's first Protestant minister to the Indians, Isaac McCoy, and his wife set up a mission school in Fort Wayne. The Reverend McCoy wrote: "We commenced with ten English scholars, six French, eight Indians and one Negro.... Besides the care of eight Indian children and six of our own, the whole charge of the family, consisting of about twenty, devolved on Mrs. McCoy; she also endeavored to instruct neighboring Indian families in the art of knitting and other domestic labors."

After one of the Indian women had been baptized, "a religious person rebuked her for wearing trinkets in her ears. She replied, 'My religion is not in my ears, it is in my heart.... Nevertheless I will ask missionaries and if they say it is wrong I will put them away.' We never deemed it necessary to make innovations on the customs of the Indians merely for the sake of form or fashion. . . . She was . . . told that the Great Spirit had not directed what should be the fashion of our dress."

The Indians badly needed such friends as the McCoys. Between 1812 and 1830, it is estimated, five hundred Miami alone were killed in drunken brawls, brought on by the liquor white men were anxious to trade them. The old Indian ways of hunting, fishing, and light farming were being destroyed by the wave of settlement, and yet for the most part they were not able to adapt to the new way of life.

In 1820 the Delaware left Indiana. The Potawatomi were driven out in 1838. The last Potawatomi village was near present-day Plymouth. The trip west was so difficult that scarcely a night's camp was made without several burials of those who had died along what came to be called the Trail of Tears.

By 1838 the Miamis had parted with most of their lands in Indiana, and in 1840 all of the remaining territory was ceded, except one tract for Meshingomesia's band, which chose to remain. After the Civil War, some of the remnants went to a reservation in Oklahoma, and in 1872 those who were left in Indiana divided the land. Their descendants are Indiana citizens today.

By 1846 most of the Indians had been driven out of "Indian-a." While this seems harsh, someone has said, "To restrain the tides of immigrants to preserve the wilderness empire of a few thousand primitive people would have been a strange reversal of history."

The brand-new capital, Indianapolis, was occupied by the state government in 1825. This was not a very magnificent removal. Only four wagons were required to transport all the property of the state.

NEW MELODIES FROM NEW HARMONY

In that same year, another new community, New Harmony, had begun its extraordinary existence.

The older Harmonie had been founded by religious leader George Rapp, whose followers were called Rappites—German people origi-

This labyrinth at New Harmony was designed by founder George Rapp.

nally from Württemberg. They bought 30,000 acres (12,140 hectares) of land in Posey County and moved there in 1815. They believed in what might be called "Christian communism," and marriage was forbidden.

These hard-working German people transformed the wilderness to a settled community. Because they felt that Rapp had been given divine inspiration, they followed his harsh discipline gladly and accomplished almost unbelievable things in clearing land, draining swamps, and constructing large brick houses and public buildings, some of which are still in good condition.

After ten years, however, the Rappites became discontented and sold all of their Harmonie holdings to an Englishman, Robert Owen.

The attention Owen gave to his workers' welfare was so unusual in those harsh days that he gained an international reputation, along with great wealth. Owen was one of the first to believe that society could improve itself through the careful planning and efforts of men of ability and good will.

He renamed Harmonie "New Harmony" because he expected to establish a perfect society of people who worked together in a new harmony of understanding. To work out his plans, he persuaded people of very unusual ability to make their homes in the Indiana wilderness. In January 1826 an extraordinary group assembled on a keelboat at Pittsburgh. Famed scientists, educators, artists, philosophers, and others floated down the Ohio and up the Wabash in one of the strangest voyages of all time. This was known as the "Boatload of Knowledge."

Most New Harmony settlers failed to understand the ideals of the founder, and his aims were never realized to any great extent. Nevertheless, so many brilliant and capable people were brought to Indiana and so many of them stayed there that New Harmony has been listed among the "world villages that have made history." Here pioneer work was done in developing the kindergarten, the infant school, trade schools, public libraries, women's clubs, geology, and other sciences. Many of the people who brought this about are described in a later section.

IMPROVEMENTS AND DISAGREEMENTS

One of the longest canals ever built, and the longest on the North American continent, was begun at Fort Wayne in 1832. This was the Wabash and Erie Canal, twenty years in the building, connecting Lake Erie with the Ohio by the historic route of the Maumee and Wabash rivers and extending 460 miles (740 kilometers).

The Wabash and Erie Canal was responsible for one of the lively episodes of Indiana history—the "Irish War." Most of the laborers on the canal were from Ireland, about half from the northern counties of Ireland and half from the balance of the Emerald Isle. They brought the rivalries of the old country with them, and a good many fights broke out.

Finally, near the present city of Wabash, about three hundred of them on each side drew battle lines. Some shots had been fired when the state militia arrived in force at the opportune moment.

In 1836 the Indiana legislature passed the Internal Improvements Law. This has been called "one of the most important ever passed by any Indiana legislature." It was designed to create more canals, as well as railroads, roads, and other transportation benefits. This was much too ambitious for the new state to manage, and when depression times came the program failed and with it the state's finances.

A favored son of Indiana, William Henry Harrison, ran for the presidency in 1840. As Territorial governor, Harrison had lived in Indiana only from 1801 to 1812, but he had made many friends there. His catchy slogan, "Tippecanoe and Tyler Too," was attractive to the residents of the state where the Battle of Tippecanoe had been fought, and the vote of Indiana helped elect the retired general to the presidency.

The Mexican War of 1846 found a large percentage of Indiana men in uniform. Five thousand volunteered for wartime service, and 554 were killed.

Indiana's original state constitution of 1816 had been a good one. However, by 1851 changes were desired, and a new constitution was adopted in that year. This continues to the present time as the basic law of Indiana.

People in Indiana generally had been against slavery, although slavery in the state had not entirely disappeared until 1843. As the nation grew more and more divided on the slavery issue, many Indiana people took leadership in the Underground Railroad. Evansville, Jeffersonville, Salem, Columbus, Greensburg, Bloomington, Madison, Lafayette, Indianapolis, South Bend, Fort Wayne, Logansport, Vincennes, Terre Haute, Richmond, and smaller communities were all "depots" where black people could be sheltered and assisted in the long escape to freedom in Canada.

The Levi Coffin house at Fountain City was known as "Central Union Station of the Underground Railroad." Coffin once wrote:

36

*This portrait of
William Henry Harrison,
elected president in 1840,
was painted by E.F. Andrews.*

"The roads were always in running order ... connections good. . . .
Seldom a week passed without receiving passengers. . . . A gentle
rap at the door. . . . Outside in the cold or rain, there would be a two-
horse wagon loaded with fugitives, perhaps the greater part of them
women and children ... When they were all safely inside ... my
wife would be up and preparing victuals ... the cold and hungry
fugitives would be made confortable."

Two thousand black people found shelter in the Coffin's Quaker
home, and Levi Coffin eventually left Indiana and became an international figure in the fight to rid the world of slavery.

Indiana played an important part in the nomination and election of
that great champion of the slaves—Abraham Lincoln. Indianapolis
had wanted to be host to the 1860 Republican convention. However,
when the Indiana delegates arrived at Chicago (where the convention was held) and saw the great crowds, they knew Indianapolis was
not yet ready for such an event.

On the first ballot at the convention, Indiana gave Lincoln all of
the state's twenty-six votes. This may have been a deciding factor in
swinging the nomination to Lincoln.

IMPORTANT IN WARTIME

Lincoln spoke in Indianapolis on the day before his birthday, during his trip to the inauguration at Washington in 1861. He called for all citizens to unite to preserve the Union and the Constitution. But the call went unheeded. Civil War came on April 12, 1861, when Southern forces fired on Fort Sumter, South Carolina.

Indiana played a unique roll in the Civil War. Governor Oliver P. Morton has been called the nation's strongest Civil War governor. When the war came, Indiana responded enthusiastically to these words of the governor: "The right of secession conceded, the nation is dissolved. . . . It would not be twelve months until a project for a Pacific empire would be set on foot. . . . We should then have before us the prospect presented by the history of the petty principalities of Germany. Need I stop to argue the political, intellectual, social, and commercial death involved in this wreck and ruin?"

When President Lincoln called for volunteers, Indiana responded so forcefully that the state quota was reached in only five days. Volunteers were trained at Camp Morton, the converted grounds of the Indiana State Fair.

As the war went on, Governor Morton's task became harder. A large part of the Indiana population either had come from the South originally or had Southern ties. The principal outlet for the products of Indiana was in the South, and the war greatly affected the economic prosperity of the state. Many became uneasy.

Because of this and other discouragements, and because of the unpopularity of the draft and Governor Morton's forceful actions, Indiana elected a Democratic legislature in 1862. When the legislature tried to limit the governor's powers, the Republican members called their plans treason, and Republicans bolted the legislature. In this way no bills could be passed, for want of a quorum. This left Governor Morton with no appropriation of funds to run the state. In a move unique in history, on his personal credit the governor borrowed funds from James J.D. Lanier of Madison, a member of the firm of Winslow, Lanier, and Company of New York, to carry on the Indiana war effort and state government.

Some of these difficulties may have been caused by Governor Morton himself. He was inclined to believe that anyone who opposed him was guilty of treason. Civil rights in Indiana were almost suspended during the Civil War. Many loyal people were harshly treated because they had ideas different from the administration's in regard to the war or slavery or other issues. Indiana's United States senator, Jesse D. Bright, was removed from the Senate in 1862 because of his friendship for the South.

In general, however, the state was one of the most important in support of the Union effort, with its great resources of food and materials.

Indiana was one of the few Northern states in which a Civil War battle actually took place. There had been fear of invasion of Indiana in 1862, and in July 18 of that year, Confederates raided Newburgh (Warwick County). In June 1863, Captain Thomas Hines crossed the Ohio near Cannelton and made his way as far north as Paoli and Hardinsburg. He and his men returned to the Ohio near Leavenworth, where most were captured. However, Captain Hines escaped by a spectacular swim across the mighty river.

Hines was an officer of the famed Confederate raider General John Hunt Morgan. In July 1863, Morgan himself crossed the Ohio from Brandenburg, Kentucky, with a force of 3,000 cavalrymen. No Southerner had dared advance so far into Northern territory. The people of Indiana were stirred as seldom before. Within two days, 20,000 volunteers had assembled at Indianapolis to repel the invaders. Another 45,000 were being readied if needed.

Morgan temporarily took Paoli and Greenville and swept on through the state. No one was sure of his destination, and the Indiana guards sought in vain to make contact with him. Morgan sallied back and forth, zigzagging from one place to another to throw pursuers off the track.

At Corydon, a small force of four hundred volunteers fought to hold off the much larger Confederate army. Three of the defenders were killed and two wounded, while eight of Morgan's men were killed in the only battle of the Civil War in Indiana. In order to save the Salem mills from being burned by the raiders, each of the two

Morgan's Raiders left such destruction as this, recreated in the movie, Guns of September.

millers was asked to pay $1,000. In his haste, one of the millers gave General Morgan $1,200. The gallant general returned the extra $200.

His pursuers close behind but never quite catching up, General Morgan went eastward into Ohio, leaving behind in Indiana about $500,000 in damages and a host of often-repeated tales by those who survived the invasion.

One of these stories concerns the pretty daughter of a Dupont meat packer, F.F. Mayfield. Mayfield's daughter scolded a Southern soldier for the theft of a large number of hams to feed the rebel forces. The Southerner is reported to have said, "You sure are purty, Ma'am, when you're in a temper. After we lick you Yanks I'll come back and marry you." He did come back, and they were married. Their descendants still live in the Dupont region.

If General Morgan had known how weak the defenses of Indianapolis were, he might have captured the capital city, freeing six thousand Confederate prisoners held there. The effect of such a victory might have been disastrous for the Northern cause. However, Morgan confined his raids to the southern part of the state.

Indiana troops fought in 308 engagements of the Civil War. The grim figures show that the Civil War cost the lives of about twice as many Indianans as were lost in both world wars later on. Altogether, 208,367 Indianans are listed as having served in the Civil War. Of that number, 24,416 were killed or died as a result of the war.

One Indianan who was in a sense a casualty of the war was President Abraham Lincoln. As the mournful funeral train passed across the country, the body of the martyred president was brought to the capitol at Indianapolis. There, while the figure beloved by so many lay in state, the throngs of people passed by to express their grief.

Indiana soldiers at General McClelland's headquarters, as recreated in the movie, Guns of September.

MODERN INDIANA

During the Civil War, Indianapolis and other cities had prospered greatly. In the post-war period Indiana enjoyed the contributions of thousands of immigrants from the Old World. Germans and Irish came in the largest numbers. England, Scotland, Hungary, Poland, France, Italy, Austria, Russia, and Canada were all represented. A wealth of many cultures and backgrounds made Indiana one of the most typically American of all the states.

Interesting events were taking place. The present state capitol was begun in 1878 and finished ten years later. Wabash is said to have become the world's first electrically lighted city in 1880. The first night baseball game in history is claimed for Fort Wayne on June 2, 1883. The first "modern" automobile chugged over the roads of Kokomo in 1894.

In 1916, Indiana celebrated the centennial of its statehood. As part of the celebration, the Daughters of the American Revolution sponsored a contest for the design of a state flag. The prize-winning design by Paul Hadley of Mooresville was officially adopted in 1917.

World War I saw the participation of 130,670 Indianans. James Bethel Gresham of Evansville is listed as one of the first three Americans to lose their lives in action in that conflict.

An unhappy development in the ten years following the war was the growth of the Ku Klux Klan in Indiana, where it was particularly successful. The Klan was opposed to blacks, Catholics, and Jews. One of the most influential Klan leaders was known as "I Am the Law" Stephenson. He was sentenced to a life term for murdering a young woman. The *Indianapolis Times* won the 1928 Pulitzer Prize for its campaign against the Ku Klux Klan.

The worst flood in the history of the Ohio River up to that time devastated most of the Indiana river communities in 1937. Some towns, such as Jeffersonville, were almost completely under water.

In the holocaust of World War II, 10,000 Indianans lost their lives, from among the total 338,000 who served.

The war greatly accelerated manufacturing throughout the state, and this trend continued. The 1970 census showed that two-thirds of

42

Burns Harbor, the first public port in Indiana, opened in 1970.

the population were city dwellers and only one-third lived in the country. This was a remarkable change from the simple rural life of the pioneer state.

Of great concern to the people of Indiana and the nation was use of the shore of Lake Michigan. Large numbers felt the irreplaceable dunes area should be preserved as a national park, while others felt that a deep-water port must be created at Burns Ditch.

This first public port in the state opened in 1970. However, to help preserve the unique dune lands, the Indiana Dunes National Lakeshore was created. Expanded in 1976, it is scheduled for long-term development.

Indiana people have long been known as Hoosiers. There are many explanations of how this word came into being, but no one is certain about it. Jacob P. Dunn, perhaps the best authority, says that it comes from *hoozer,* used in England, and means "hill dweller."

Many people outside the state think "Hoosier" has uncomplimentary meanings, of a rustic or peasant, but to the people of Indiana "Hoosier" stands for "gracious and kind, a proud word conjuring up someone who has roots and belongs to the forests, trees, rivers, and lakes of the state." The people of Indiana are Hoosiers and proud of it!

Golden raintrees, brought from Asia, now grow widely in southern Indiana.

Natural Treasures

PLANTS AND ANIMALS

Side by side in the wonderful dunes region of Indiana grow the white lizard tail, a tropical plant, and bog callas from the far north. The rare natural mingling of tropical and arctic plants is only one of the reasons the dunes rate so highly as a natural treasure. Here, too, may be found arctic lichen, the semi-tropical pawpaw and prickly pear cactus of the desert, orchids, iris, and many other rare, interesting plants and ferns. First to bloom in the spring is the delicate trailing arbutus, sometimes bursting out at the edge of a snowdrift.

Among the rarest plants of other Indiana regions are two carniverous (meat eating) plants of the Limberlost area. These are the round-leafed sundew and the pitcher plant. The sundew captures insects with a sticky coating on the leaf, which then folds up and digests the unlucky bug. Unwary insects are lured into the pitcher plant's pitcher, where they are drowned and digested.

Jack-in-the-pulpit, blue lupine, rue anemone, violet, hepatica, marshmarigold, ox-eyed daisy, goldenrod, asters, sunflowers, and the wild carrot are common Indiana plants. Peony is officially the state flower, adopted by the General Assembly in 1957. The dark fruit of elderberry and the cheery orange-red berry of bittersweet are familiar and well-loved symbols of the growing things of Indiana.

One hundred thirty-four tree species are native to Indiana, and the tulip is the state tree. This now comparatively rare tree once was the mighty monarch of pioneer forests. The massive sycamores so typical of the state are especially impressive to visitors. Southern persimmon, black gum, southern cypress, northern tamarack, bog willow— all may be found. Typical of Indiana's climate and locale are oak, walnut, hickory, beech, maple, ash, catalpa, and elm.

From faraway China and Korea, William Maclure brought the "Tree of the Golden Rain" to New Harmony. The community is now often visited for the beauty of its many blooming golden raintrees. They spread widely over southern Indiana, and are now commonly planted in other parts of the state.

Buffalo, once numerous in Indiana, are now honored in the state seal.

More than fourteen kinds of animals that were common in pioneer days have almost vanished from Indiana. These include the bear, buffalo, and wildcat, although there is a domesticated herd of buffalo in Pokagon State Park. A few wolves and coyotes remain in isolated regions. Red fox, muskrat, raccoon, woodchuck, rabbit, opossum, mink, and squirrel are found in varying numbers.

Three hundred and twenty species of birds were common in Indiana in 1900, although many were migratory. At the present time fewer than half of those 320 are known in the state. Some of them are rarely seen.

Pike, catfish, bass, sunfish, and pickerel are common fish.

MINERAL WEALTH

The greatest mineral wealth nature has given to Indiana comes from the remains of ancient plants and animals. Limestone was formed from the hardened skeletons of marine creatures of ancient times. Reserves of limestone in Indiana are large. Indiana's oolitic limestone is one of the world's finest building stones. Coal is formed from the petrified remains of ancient plant life.

Oil is found in at least sixty-two Indiana counties, and there is still some natural gas.

Sedimentary rocks, sandstone, gypsum, shale, clay, kaolin, sand and gravel, all are abundantly available in Indiana.

46

People Use Their Treasures

MANUFACTURING: SOUND THE TRUMPETS

Indiana leads all the states in the production of musical instruments, prefabricated buildings, and biological products. It ranks second in book printing, veneer mills, production of storage batteries, and wood office furniture. Only two other states produce more steel products, aircraft equipment, pharmaceuticals, electric motors, and generators.

One of the most important manufacturing centers of the world is the Calumet area in northwestern Indiana. The steel mills at Gary are among the largest in the world, and many other operations there make this one of the greatest concentrations of industry anywhere.

The annual report of United States Steel Company once stated, "It has been decided to construct and put in operation a new plant to be located on the south shore of Lake Michigan in Calumet Township, Lake County, Indiana, and a large acreage of land has been purchased for that purpose." At that time Gary did not exist. It was named in honor of Judge Elbert H. Gary, chairman of the steel company. He had much responsibility for planning the new plant and

Molten metal casts an eerie glow at U.S. Steel's Gary plant.

Indiana is a leader in the manufacture of musical instruments.
Here, at the Kimball Piano plant, an employee helps create a piano.

new community. Today Gary is the second city in population in Indiana and is the largest city in the United States to be founded during the twentieth century. By 1929, less than twenty-five years after Gary's founding, steel had become the largest industry in Indiana.

Indiana has unusual importance to the world's musicians. Sixty percent of all band instruments are said to be manufactured at Elkhart, "band instrument capital of the world."

Elkhart is also home of Miles Laboratories, one of the country's leading pharmaceutical houses.

Manufacturing in South Bend had early beginnings in the wagons of the Studebakers, Oliver plows, and Singer sewing machines. Although the Studebaker-Packard Company still maintains its headquarters in South Bend, the manufacture of Studebaker automobiles there was concluded in 1964. This ended sixty-five years of automobile production which began in 1899, when Studebaker first manufactured bodies for electric automobiles. Other automobiles once manufactured in Indiana include the well-known Auburn, Overland, Stutz, Duesenberg, Cord, and the not-so-well-known Lexington, made at Connorsville. In 1965 an Indianapolis firm began production of a new version of the renowned Duesenberg.

The Oliver Company at South Bend continues to be one of the country's leading agricultural equipment companies.

Manufacture of automobile parts and equipment and supplies related to the automobile industry is especially important in Indiana. General Motors and its subsidiaries employ more people than any firm in the state. The Guide Lamp Corporation at Anderson is the world's largest manufacturer of auto lighting equipment. Fire trucks are also produced at Anderson. Bendix Products, an automotive firm at South Bend, is almost a city in itself.

Fort Wayne is known as the world center of gasoline-pump manufacture. The city's leadership in this field began when Sylvanus F. Bowser perfected a self-measuring tank for kerosene. This developed into the well-known filling-station pump of today.

Kokomo claims to be the birthplace of the "modern" automobile and the pneumatic rubber tire. Wayne Mills at Fort Wayne produced the first "full-fashion" hosiery made in the United States. A large percentage of the world's diamond tools are also made in Fort Wayne. About 80 percent of all magnets made in this country are produced in the Indiana Steel Products Division of Indiana General Corporation at Valparaiso.

Indianapolis is called Telephone Capital of the World, producing millions of telephones a year at the Western Electric Indianapolis Works. Since 1950 the plant has made over 100 million telephones, and is the only plant making telephones for the Bell system.

Anderson claims to be the largest manufacturer of files in the world, and Madison is a center for decorative wrought iron. Madison was one of the early Indiana manufacturing centers, with a paper mill as early as 1828.

The Ball Brothers plant at Muncie is one of the largest manufacturers of glass containers in the world.

USING THE MINERAL WEALTH

Limestone quarrying and "working" is one of the foremost industries of Indiana. Bedford limestone has become one of the best-known construction materials anywhere. It is especially noteworthy for its ability to take fine chiseling and carving. Dr. Winthrop Foote of Bedford was one of the first to see the possibilities of the stone, and persuaded the first stonecutter to start his business there. Dr. Foote and his brother further showed their interest in the region's limestone by having their tomb carved into a single boulder of the material. This can still be seen at Bedford.

Eighty percent of all United States "dimensional" limestone is quarried in the Bedford-Bloomington region. The famed stone has been used in the Empire State Building at New York, the Chicago Art Institute, the World War Memorial at Indianapolis, and many another noted structure.

Coal, cement, and petroleum rank ahead of stone in annual dollar value of product in Indiana, with coal continuing to be the leading mineral product of the state. Large-scale coal mining began in Indiana in 1857. Over 25 million short tons (22,679,625 metric tons) of coal are produced in Indiana each year.

Petroleum and gas are important to the Indiana economy. As early as 1890, 63,000 barrels (8,595 metric tons) of oil were produced there. In 1963 over 5,000 wells in the state produced at the rate of 11,417,000 barrels (1,557,572 metric tons). The state's refineries also produce a very large volume. The American Oil Company refinery at Whiting is one of the largest in the world. It produces possibly the largest variety of petroleum products of any refinery, with products ranging from the finest oil for watches to the heaviest lubricant for great Diesel engines.

Natural gas was discovered at Portland and Anderson in 1886. Free gas was offered to factories to induce them to locate at Portland, and because the supply was considered unlimited, it was squandered in other ways. Carefully used, this gas might have lasted a century. The story was the same at Muncie, where gas torches burned in the streets and no one bothered to turn out the gas lights.

AGRICULTURE

In the early days, a favorite quotation was "Crops were so heavy that's what gives rise to stories about earthquakes."

50

Although only a small percentage of Indiana people now live on farms such as this one, the state ranks between sixth and eighth in agricultural income.

Today's crops continue to be "heavy."

Although a small percentage of Indianans now live on farms, agricultural products are valued at more than $3 billion yearly. Of this, by far the largest part comes from livestock, primarily hogs. Indiana generally ranks between sixth and eighth among the states in agricultural income.

Corn is Indiana's main crop, and the state ranks third, behind Iowa and Illinois, in the nation's corn production. Some years Indiana gains first rank in popcorn production. The state is second or third in soybeans, third in tomatoes for processing, third in hogs, and third in mint for oils. In distilling spearmint and peppermint oils, Indiana ranks first.

The Madison area is known for its tobacco crop, and Richmond is noted for its large rose-growing industry. The vegetable greenhouses of Terre Haute are among the world's largest.

TRANSPORTATION AND COMMUNICATION

Since the time of the early canoes of the Indian and European on the many rivers, water transportation has been important in Indiana. The Ohio River formed a broad highway on which settlers and their goods drifted on flatboats toward their new homes. The flatboat men were among the most colorful in our history.

In 1811 the first steamboat puffed along Indiana's Ohio River shores, and by 1820 had reached the internal rivers. The growth of river traffic is shown by the fact that only twenty years later, between March 1 and April 16, 1831, fifty-four steamboats called at Vincennes alone. Terre Haute became an important terminal of the New Orleans trade.

Indiana's river shipyards were busy. Jeffersonville built two thousand steamboats, including many famous ones. Between 1830 and 1860 the shipyards at New Albany were turning out such prominent boats as the *Eclipse* and the *Robert E. Lee*. The coming of the showboat, a complete floating theater, was an occasion for excitement in river communities.

Today, shipments on the Ohio River are the heaviest in history as busy towboats cut through the waters, propelling barges carrying spectacular loads, such as multi-storied automobile carriers. The American Commercial Barge Line, with its terminal at Jefferson-

The Delta Queen, *shown here at Madison, continues the sternwheel tradition.*

ville, is one of the world's largest river transportation companies. Evansville, Mt. Vernon, and Jeffersonville are important freight-handling centers.

To the north, Lake Michigan ports have played an important role in transportation. In the 1840s, Michigan City was a busier lake port than Chicago. With the opening of the St. Lawrence Seaway, Indiana now can receive oceangoing ships in any ports suitable for handling them. Because increased capacity for this traffic is of great value to Indiana, the port at Burns Ditch was created.

Land travel in early Indiana was difficult and tedious. The first wheeled vehicle in Indiana, in fact in the whole Northwest Territory, is said to have been the two-wheeled French *caleche,* made entirely of wood.

One of the federal government's first great road-building projects was the National Road, built from 1829 through 1839. This crossed the state from Richmond to Terre Haute, by way of Indianapolis.

The Maples Tavern near present Dublin was a typical stop on the old National Road. As many as twelve stagecoaches in one day might pause there for fresh horses while the passengers ate and drank and brought the news from the East. The better stage lines are said to have been so punctual that the bugle notes announcing a coach's arrival could be depended on for the time of day.

The story is told of President Martin Van Buren's making a stagecoach tour over the National Road. His stage overturned near Plainfield. Van Buren had vetoed a road repair bill, and there may have been a plot to wreck his stage, to show him how much the road needed repairing. In any event, there was a crowd on hand to watch the wreck, and the nearby tree came to be known as the Van Buren Elm.

The Buffalo Trace Road from New Albany to Vincennes is said to have followed the trail made by buffalo. Other early roads included the Michigan Road, built by the state from Michigan City to Madison on the Ohio River. It crossed the National Road at Indianapolis.

Indianapolis is improving its position as a leading crossroad as the national program of interstate highways is completed. The city is or will be at the intersection of seven of these routes, the greatest concentration of such superhighways in the nation.

The first railroad in Indiana was a stretch of experimental track at Shelbyville, built in 1834 and only a little more than a mile (1.6 kilometers) in length. Its one coach was drawn by a horse. The first railroad with a steam locomotive was begun at Madison in 1838. Its ascent up Madison Hill from the Ohio Valley is the world's steepest without cogs or cable. The tracks reached Columbus in 1844, and in 1847 a splendid celebration was held at Indianapolis when the tracks reached there. Today's railroad mileage in Indiana is more than 12,200 (19,600 kilometers). The first "belt" railroad in the country was built to handle freight around Indianapolis.

Indianapolis also became the world's greatest inter-urban center. In 1893 one of the first electric inter-urban coaches ran between Brazil and Harmony, and for many years inter-urban transportation in Indiana grew. Indiana had 2,137 miles (3,439.2 kilometers) of mainline inter-urban track. In 1910, four hundred trains per day used the Indianapolis terminal.

In communications, the first telegraph office was opened at Vincennes in 1847.

Vincennes was also the home of the first newspaper in Indiana— the Indiana *Gazette,* established in 1804.

Early newspapermen often had difficult times. The *Dog Fennel Gazette* of Rushville was printed on only one side of the paper. Each subscriber then returned the paper so it could be printed on the other side. Today, the *Indianapolis Star* and *News* are the largest newspapers in the state.

Human Treasures

Indiana has one of the most remarkable records of all the states in the number and variety of people of national and international renown who have been associated with the state. This is even more remarkable because of Indiana's relatively short history and the many writings that picture Indiana as a little "backwoodsy."

A POOR MIGRANT FAMILY

Not long after Indiana became a state in 1816, a father, mother, and two children, a boy and girl, crossed the Ohio River from Kentucky and arrived at Cannelton. They borrowed a heavy vehicle and a team of oxen from nearby settler Francis Posey to move their household goods to the 160-acre (64.7-hectare) Little Pigeon Creek farm the father had applied for. There was no road, and two days were required to force their way over the 16 miles (25.7 kilometers) of wilderness.

This was the Thomas and Nancy Hanks Lincoln family. Their seven-year-old son, Abraham, was destined to become one of the most universally known persons in history. Such great fame would have seemed unbelievable to the simple family as they huddled through the winter in a lean-to shelter. Because it was too late to plant crops, they lived on wild game and water from melted snow.

For fourteen years the family lived in the Little Pigeon Creek region, while Abraham Lincoln grew to manhood. Thomas Lincoln meant well, but he has been called "improvident."

In October 1818, Nancy Hanks Lincoln became gravely ill with "milk sick" and died. ("Milk sick" is a poisoning, caused by a substance in white snakeroot. The poison is passed to humans in milk from cows which have eaten the snakeroot. Most patients recover but some die.) About a year later, Thomas Lincoln married Sarah Bush Johnson, who encouraged her stepson Abraham in his fierce desire to learn and get an education. Thomas Lincoln did not approve of this. Nevertheless, with only about a year of formal

Abraham Lincoln spent fourteen years of his boyhood at this farm, now preseved as the Lincoln Boyhood National Memorial.

schooling, Abraham set about to read everything available within 50 miles (80.5 kilometers) of the pioneer community. He often walked the 17 miles (27.3 kilometers) to Rockport to borrow books from John Pitcher's law library. He was familiar with every legal document he could find to read, including the statutes of Indiana, the Declaration of Independence, and the constitutions of the United States and Indiana.

Abraham removed brush, cut grain with a sickle, threshed, split rails, and became skilled at carpentry and cabinet making. Often his father hired him out to neighbors at twenty-five cents per day as hostler, wood chopper, ploughman, carpenter, or even baby-sitter. He also operated a ferry at Anderson.

Abraham was extremely popular and went to great lengths to be liked by everyone. Once, when he caught some boys in his watermelon patch, he is said to have perched on the rail fence, and told them stories while they all ate watermelon. Young and old loved to hear his jokes, recitations, and imitations.

By the time the Lincoln family left the Lincoln country of Indiana in 1830, a perceptive observer might have predicted that the young man of the family would go far, in spite of the handicaps of his primitive upbringing—perhaps even because of them.

INDIANA CHIEFS

A number of Indiana Indian chiefs deserve an outstanding place in American history. Foremost of these might be the Shawnee chief, Tecumseh. Historian R.E. Banta has called Tecumseh "one of America's truly great men." Other historians have described him as "fearless, upright, generous ... with a deep love for his troubled race."

He hoped to persuade his people to give up liquor, combine their strength through confederation, drive the white man out of their lands, and return to the old ways of their fathers. The tide of history, of course, was against Tecumseh in this, but his honorable ways and vast ability gained the respect of even his bitterest foes.

Tecumseh's half-brother was almost as remarkable, although not so admirable as Tecumseh. This was Tenskwatawa, a one-eyed man of great physical strength, generally known as the Prophet. He and Tecumseh were born in Ohio, but in 1808 they established their headquarters, Prophetstown, on the Wabash River at the mouth of the Tippecanoe River. The Prophet claimed to have had a vision of the new life for his Indian people, and he preached the theories of Tecumseh with fierce and persuasive oratory. He was a great foe of Christian teachings.

When Governor Harrison heard of this, he said, "Who is this pretended prophet who dares speak in the name of the Great Creator? If God has really employed him, He doubtless has authorized him to perform miracles. If he really is a prophet, ask him to cause the sun to stand still—the moon to alter its course—the rivers to cease to flow—or the dead to arise from their graves. If he does these things, you may then believe that he has been sent from God."

The Prophet accepted Harrison's challenge and boldly announced that on June 16, 1806, at noon he would blot out the sun and cause darkness. Of course, he had learned of a coming eclipse of the sun, but his superstitious followers were greatly impressed when his prediction came true.

In the end, of course, he was defeated by Harrison at Tippecanoe. When Tecumseh returned from the south after the battle, he

The Shawnee Tenskwatawa, known as the Prophet, was the brother of the great Shawnee chief, Tecumseh. Painting by Charles Bird King.

"found the work of ten years in ruins," and the great dreams both he and his brother had for their people never came true.

More realistic was Chief Meshekinnoquah, or "Little Turtle," whose village was on the Eel River, near what is now Columbia City. He fought the white men with great military ability. In a battle at Fort Wayne, his forces killed 180 American troops. Later, just over the Ohio border east of Portland, about 1,000 warriors under Little Turtle attacked the army of General Arthur St. Clair, killing 632 and wounding 300, one of the greatest defeats ever suffered by United States forces. It was planned and carried out by Little Turtle and his adopted white son, William Wells.

Later, however, both Little Turtle and Wells realized that the tide of white settlers could not be avoided, and Wells left him for a while and fought on the whites' side in the Battle of Fallen Timbers. Little Turtle signed the Treaty of Green Ville, saying, "I have been the last to sign this treaty; I will be the last to break it." He kept his word.

He and Wells visited the "Great White Father," George Washington, who gave the chief a sword and commissioned famed artist Gilbert Stuart to paint his portrait. Little Turtle also paid visits to Presidents John Adams and Thomas Jefferson. He disregarded Tecumseh and remained a friend of the Americans.

When Little Turtle died on July 14, 1812, he was given a military funeral by the American troops. William Wells was sent to help evacuate Fort Dearborn, where Chicago now is, and he was killed when the Indians massacred that garrison on August 15, 1812.

James Logan, a nephew of Tecumseh, died fighting for the American side in the War of 1812. Logansport is named in his honor. Last of the Miami war chiefs was Francis Godfroy. A French nobleman named Godfroy had married an Indian, and the Indian family took his name. Francis Godfroy became very wealthy by operating a trading post, where he lived in feudal splendor. He was said to be "generous and fearless," and had great strength in an enormous physique. He weighed over 400 pounds (over 181 kilograms).

Simon Pokagon was the last chief of the Potawatomi in Indiana. He became well known for his writing of Indian history and poetry.

Mishawaka was named for an Indian princess. An interesting story is that of Frances Slocum, "White Rose of the Miamis," who was abducted by Indians and lived her long life as an Indian woman and wife of a chief.

LITERARY LEADERS

Indiana has produced an extraordinary number of well-known writers. Some wrote almost entirely about the state they knew so well, while others wrote of strange and faraway people and places. Probably the best known for re-creating the Indiana of the past and the common people of the state was the "Hoosier Poet," James Whitcomb Riley, who was born in a log cabin at Greenfield. He gained his first fame in the form of notoriety because of a literary hoax.

Riley wrote a poem in the style of Edgar Allan Poe, called it "Leonainie," and passed this off as an unpublished work of Poe. When the hoax was discovered, Riley was widely denounced, but the fact that he could write such a poem was never forgotten. A vast number of his poems appeared in the newspapers of Indiana. His poems were loved by the average man, and "Little Orphant Annie," "The Old Swimmin' Hole," and "The Raggedy Man" are still widely read.

The first Indiana writer able to create a feeling of frontier life in his works was Edward Eggleston of Vevay on the Ohio. His *The Hoosier Schoolmaster* made him famous, and his *The Beginners of a Nation* has been called "one of the most important pioneer works in American social history."

Gene Stratton Porter, born near Wabash, became the most successful writer of her day in terms of the sales of her books. She wrote mainly light fiction about the Limberlost region of her state, in such books as *A Girl of the Limberlost*.

Theodore Dreiser was born in Terre Haute. His *A Hoosier Holiday* is a series of sketches of Indiana boyhood, delightful portraits of the Midwest. His best-known work is *An American Tragedy*.

A writer of far different works and yet long a dean of Indiana authors was Newton Booth Tarkington, born at Indianapolis in 1869. He was twice winner of the Pulitzer Prize for his novels *The Magnificent Ambersons* and *Alice Adams*. His most popular book is probably his novel of adolescence, *Seventeen*.

Meredith Nicholson won fame for his romantic novels, such as *The House of a Thousand Candles,* as did Charles Major for *When Knighthood Was in Flower,* and Maurice Thompson of Crawfordsville for *Alice of Old Vincennes.*

George Ade is known for his "typical" Indiana characters and situations in such books as *Fables in Slang*. Other significant Indiana authors are David Graham Phillips and George B. McCutcheon.

Some of America's leading historians and sociologists are associated with Indiana. Albert J. Beveridge was senator from Indiana for twelve years. He won the Pulitzer Prize for his biography, *John Marshall*. Noted historian Charles Austin Beard was a graduate of DePauw University. With his wife Mary he wrote *The Rise of American Civilization* and other brilliant works of social history. Another husband and wife team, Robert and Helen Lynd, chose Muncie for

Booth Tarkington, prominent Indiana author, won two Pulitzer Prizes. Painting by James Montgomery Flagg.

sociological studies of a typical small city. They published their findings in *Middletown* and later *Middletown in Transition*. Other prominent Indiana nonfiction writers are Claude Bowers and John C. Redpath.

Two leading Indiana journalists were Berry Sulgrove of Indianapolis and Ernie Pyle of Dana. Pyle was probably the best-known newspaper correspondent of World War II. His death in action in the Pacific caused universal regret. Other prominent Indiana journalists are Roy Howard, Elmer Davis, Edwin C. Hill, and Kent Cooper.

FOUR CAREERS

A controversial figure who enjoyed four wholly different careers, Lew Wallace was born in Brookville and became lawyer, soldier, statesman, and author. Wallace began his military service at the age of nineteen in the war with Mexico. He wrote his first novel in 1853, but it was not published until much later.

61

Wallace was one of the few men who was prepared for the Civil War. Before the war came, he organized and trained a company at Crawfordsville. They were a flashy group in their colorful Zouave uniforms, giving exhibition drills all over the state.

Governor Morton appointed Wallace adjutant general of Indiana, and he later served as a brigadier general. At the age of thirty-four he became a major general, the youngest man holding that rank. In the Battle of Shiloh, General Grant felt that Wallace failed to carry out an order. Although Grant later agreed that the affair was probably a misunderstanding, this cast a cloud on Wallace's life which was never quite cleared. Later, Wallace's work during the Battle of Monacacy is said to have "saved Washington from almost certain capture." His promotion to major general was due largely to his role in the capture of Fort Donelson. He was a member of the court that tried the persons accused of plotting President Lincoln's assassination.

After the war, his career took a strange turn when he accepted a post as major general in the Mexican army.

Between these unusual phases of his work, he returned to Crawfordsville and the practice of law. In 1878, he was appointed governor of the Territory of New Mexico. While there, he wrote another novel, *Ben Hur*. This became one of the best-known literary works of all time. It has often been used in spectacular productions of stage and movies, and gave its author worldwide fame.

In 1881, President Garfield appointed Lew Wallace ambassador to Turkey, and while in Constantinople he wrote *The Prince of India*. He died at Crawfordsville in 1905.

ARTISTS AND MUSICIANS

In 1837 an English artist, George Winter, came to Indiana and even at that early date was able to support his family entirely through his art. He studied and painted the Indians and did many landscapes.

Theodore Clement Steele was born near Spencer in 1847. He began a painting career at the age of five, later studying in Chicago and in Europe at Munich. He was the originator of the Brown County Art Colony, and is said to have "brought the Hoosier State a worldwide reputation as an art center." Other noted artists include sculptor George Gray Barnard of Madison, William Merritt Chase, and Gaar Williams.

An Indiana cartoonist of worldwide reputation was Frank McKinney (Kin) Hubbard. He created the rustic philosopher Abe Martin, who has been called "one of the most beloved characters in American fiction." Will Rogers said of Hubbard, "No man in our generation was within a mile of him." Another famed cartoonist was John T. McCutcheon.

The family home of famed musical comedy writer Cole Porter was Peru. Probably his most famous numbers are "Begin the Beguine," from *Jubilee,* and "Night and Day." Another renowned Indiana popular composer, Hoagland (Hoagy) Carmichael, a native of Bloomington, created the classic "Star Dust," as well as many other hits.

Thomas Paine Westendorf, an official of the Indiana Boys' School at Plainfield, wrote the well-loved song "I'll Take You Home Again, Kathleen" when his wife was away on an extended visit.

Indiana's state song, "On the Banks of the Wabash, Far Away," and many others, were written by Paul Dresser of Terre Haute, brother of Theodore Dreiser. Paul changed his name to Dresser to join a medicine show, and in the 1890s became one of the most popular songwriters in the country. He also headed a music publishing firm.

Albert von Tilzer wrote such well-known songs as "Take Me Out to the Ball Game," "I want a Girl Just like the Girl," and "Wait till the Sun Shines, Nellie."

PUBLIC FIGURES

Thomas Beveridge, a leading Indiana statesman and historian, said of Indiana's Civil War governor Oliver P. Morton, "He was the Gibraltar of the government of the West. Stanton and Morton were the imperial wills that held aloft the hands of Lincoln until victory came. So far as deeds and facts could make it so, Morton was deputy president of the United States in active charge of the Ohio Valley. No man can tell what the results would have been had not some man like our Morton been what and where our Morton was.''

Morton was certainly one of the leading political figures of the North during the period. Few would have had the courage of Morton when he borrowed huge sums of money on his personal credit to finance Indiana during the war. It is said Morton himself considered that he saved Indiana for the Union, but it is questionable that there were very many Indianans who were truly disloyal.

In 1867, Governor Morton resigned to accept appointment as United States senator from Indiana, and served until his death in 1877. Summing up his life, historian Dr. Emma Lou Thornbrough writes, "In contrast to Lincoln, whose reputation has grown with the years, the luster of Morton's reputation has dimmed. Perhaps it is because Morton, in spite of his undoubted ability and service to the Union cause, lacked those qualities which Lincoln possessed in such great measure—magnanimity and forbearance and political genius without narrow partisanship."

Indiana cherishes its associations with the Harrison presidential family. William Henry Harrison did not go to the White House

Grouseland, the Vincennes home of William Henry Harrison.

directly from Indiana, but his grandson, Benjamin, did, although Benjamin was not born in Indiana. He came to Indianapolis in 1854 to practice law, and served in the Civil War as a general. A United States senator from Indiana, he defeated Grover Cleveland for the presidency in 1888. Except for his term as president, he lived in Indianapolis until his death in 1901.

Four vice presidents of the United States also came from Indianapolis: Schuyler Colfax, Thomas R. Marshall, Charles W. Fairbanks, and Thomas A. Hendricks.

John Hay, secretary of state under McKinley and Roosevelt and a distinguished author, was born in Salem. However, he is said to have disliked his native state intensely. He began his career as secretary to Abraham Lincoln.

Hugh McCulloch of Fort Wayne, also an author, was secretary of the treasury under Presidents Lincoln, Johnson, and Arthur, and Caleb B. Smith of Indianapolis was Lincoln's secretary of the interior. James J. Davis served as secretary of labor under Presidents Harding, Coolidge, and Hoover. He was particularly active in the development of the Loyal Order of Moose.

One of the colorful and controversial Indiana figures of the Civil War was General Ambrose E. Burnside, native of Liberty. He gave his name to the kind of brushy whiskers he wore down the sides of his face. These are correctly called "burnsides"—and incorrectly referred to as "sideburns" by reversing the general's name.

Indiana was the scene of a little-known but interesting episode in the life of General and President Ulysses S. Grant. When the Civil War came, Grant was clerking in his father's leather store in Galena, Illinois. He had resigned his army commission. On a visit to the home of his West Point classmate, General Joseph Reynolds, at Lafayette, Indiana, Grant remarked that he had been offered a colonel's commission in the army, but he no longer felt capable of commanding a thousand men. Joseph Reynold's brother, William, lectured Grant sternly: "Young man, you have been trained at the government school and at public expense, and if you don't know how to command, who does? To whom are we to look in such times of peril—can't you accept? You have got to. What's a thousand men? I give orders to that many myself. . . . Give me that telegraph blank. I will write your answer.'' He did, and Grant resumed a career that was to carry him to the White House. It is interesting to wonder what the course of United States history might have been without that telegram.

Other prominent Indiana political figures include Richard W. Thompson, Walter G. Gersham, Harry S. New, Willis Van Devanter, Will Hays, and Paul McNutt.

Wendell Lewis Willkie was the unsuccessful Republican candidate for the presidency of the United States in his campaign of 1940 against Franklin D. Roosevelt. He accepted the nomination in his native Elwood.

INDUSTRIOUS AND INVENTIVE

Charles G. Conn, a grocer at Elkhart, loved to play the cornet. When he injured his lip, he invented a mouthpiece for the instrument which still permitted him to play. So many others began to want this fine new mouthpiece that eventually Mr. Conn was manufacturing them in his home. In 1875 he rented a one-room building and began to manufacture cornets along with his mouthpiece. From that modest beginning has grown the world's largest musical instrument enterprise, still centered at Elkhart.

Another Elkhart man, Dr. Franklin Miles, set up a small business to make and market his medicines. Products of Miles Laboratories are known around the world.

The five Ball brothers were successful glass manufactures in New York. When they decided to set up a branch plant farther west, Muncie offered 70 acres (28.3 hectares) of land, free gas for fuel, and $5,000 in cash to encourage the location of the company there. So successful did the enterprise become that the Ball brothers moved their headquarters to Muncie, and their interest in Indiana has resulted in many extraordinary contributions to their adopted state.

One of these is Ball State Teachers College (now Ball State University). The Ball family purchased an abandoned college at

Muncie and presented it to the state for the training of educators. They continued to make substantial contributions to the college.

Henry and Clement Studebaker set up a factory in South Bend in 1852 to manufacture farm wagons. Large numbers of the prairie schooners which lumbered across the western plains were manufactured in the Studebaker works; then electric trucks were made, and finally the automobiles which took the Studebaker name around the world.

James Oliver began manufacturing plows in South Bend in 1855. In 1864 he discovered a method to harden steel by chilling. This permitted the use of a steel moldboard on plows so that they would remain sharp over a long period of time. The firm became a great success. The Studebaker wagon and the Oliver plow played a large part in the agricultural development of the nation.

Another of Indiana's leading industrialists was Judge Elbert Gary, founder of the steel mills and city of Gary. Judge Gary was one of the early industrialists to take great interest in workers' welfare, pension and retirement programs, loans for home ownership, and better sanitary conditions. It is said that Judge Gary contributed to every church, hospital, civic, and fraternal building erected in Gary during his lifetime.

On the Fourth of July, 1894, inventor Elwood Haynes of Kokomo towed to the edge of town a strange contraption. He had it hitched back of a horse-drawn carriage. This was the first automobile ever built with clutch system and electric ignition. Haynes described the first ride: "It moved off at once at a speed of about seven miles [11.3 kilometers] per hour and was driven about one and one-half miles [2.4 kilometers] into the country. It was then turned around and ran all the way back into the city without making a single stop." As they approached a small hill, Elmer Apperson, who was riding with Haynes, said, "I wonder if the little devil can make the hill?" They both laughed with pleasure when the car chugged laboriously over the moderate slope.

Of course, many automobiles had been made throughout the world at much earlier dates, but the Haynes car holds high rank in automotive history because of its mechanical success and because it

The print shop of Elihu Stout, in Vincennes. Stout, who established the first newspaper in Indiana, was also the first printer in the state.

was the first car to be essentially complete, as we know the internal combustion engine automobile today.

George H. Hammond, for whom Hammond is named, was the originator of refrigeration of freight cars for transport of meat and produce. His meat-packing plant was the first industry in Hammond. E. Gurney Hill, of Hill Floral Products Company, Richmond, was noted for his origination and development of new kinds of roses. Wilbur Wright, co-inventor of the airplane, was born near New Castle, but the family did not remain long in Indiana after his birth.

Richard J. Gatling, Eli Lilly, Carl Fisher, and Bernard Gimbel are other inventors and business people of note.

A HARMONIOUS CHORUS: GENIUS AT NEW HARMONY

Although Robert Owen was not successful in creating the ideal community at New Harmony, he did encourage the assembling of a remarkable group of talented people at New Harmony. These included his four sons, Robert Dale Owen, William Owen, Richard Owen, and David Dale Owen.

68

Robert Dale Owen served in the United States Congress, where he introduced the bill to use the long-neglected bequest of Englishman James Smithson to establish the Smithsonian Institution. In 1862 he wrote a letter to President Lincoln urging him to free the Southern slaves. Lincoln said of this powerful document, "Its perusal stirred me like a trumpet call." Five days later, Lincoln made the momentous decision to issue his Emancipation Proclamation.

David Dale Owen became one of the leading scientists of the United States. He was United States Geologist, and New Harmony was headquarters for the United States Geological Survey until it was moved to Washington.

Constance Fauntleroy, an Owen descendant, founded the first formally organized women's club in the United States at New Harmony in 1859. This was based on the first women's literary club, which had been founded earlier at New Harmony by Frances Wright.

Other New Harmony leaders were William Maclure, humanitarian and advocate of education and libraries, and artist Charles Alexander Le Sueur.

SUCH INTERESTING PEOPLE

James J.D. Lanier was living in New York during the Civil War, but he had such faith in the war effort and in his home state of Indiana that as the war went on he gave unsecured loans of a million dollars to the state to help finance Indiana's war effort. His faith was rewarded and the money eventually repaid.

Others were not so fortunate. Francis Vigo, who helped outfit the troops of George Rogers Clark, was not repaid during his lifetime. Father Pierre Gibault, who aided the American effort, was refused the small claim of $1,500 and 2 acres (.8 hectare) of land. Clark was not successful in his real estate business at Clarksville, and he died a broken and unhappy man. General recognition of his great contributions did not come until long after his death.

Dr. John Evans of Attica predicted to friends that he would become wealthy, would build a city, found a college, govern a state, and be a United States senator. Much of his strange prediction came true. He was one of the founders of Northwestern University at Evanston, Illinois, which city was named in his honor. He was territorial governor of Colorado, and when Colorado petitioned to become a state, Evans was named senator, although statehood was not granted then, and he did not take his seat. But he did help found the University of Colorado and he became a railroad president.

Other Indiana physicians had outstanding careers. Dr. George Frederick Dick and his wife, Dr. Gladys Dick, developed the Dick test for scarlet fever, and Dr. William Trafton discovered a cure for milk sickness, which had claimed, among many others, the life of Abraham Lincoln's mother.

Another unusual medical man was Dr. E.M.C. Neyman of Livonia, who practiced medicine until the age of ninety-six. He claimed to be the son of Marshal Ney, one of Napoleon's generals.

Ben Wallace of Peru and a partner bought a traveling carnival. Its principal assets were an elephant named Diamond and a one-eyed lion. There were also two monkeys, a horse, and a camel. They trained the elephant in a railroad roundhouse and gave their show in Peru. This was the start of the Hagenbeck-Wallace Circus, one of the world's largest.

Ann Ellsworth of Lafayette had an unusual distinction. Samuel F.B. Morse had told Miss Ellsworth while he was working on the telegraph that if he were successful, he would let her select the first words to go over the wire. It was Miss Ellsworth who selected the famous phrase "What hath God wrought?"

Among other interesting people of Indiana were Christopher Harrison of Salem, the recluse who became lieutenant governor; Alice of Old Vincennes, who hid the French flag from "Hair Buyer" Hamilton; eccentric Mary Wright, who for forty years gave piano concerts for her neighbors in a log cabin at Vevay; "Diana of the Dunes," the female hermit who scampered unclothed across the sands; Gilbert Vestison, "Hermit of the Knobs"; and lovely motion picture star Carole Lombard, native of Fort Wayne.

Other interesting Indiana people include John (Ole) Olsen, Kenesaw Mountain Landis, Knute Rockne, and Wilbur Shaw.

70

Teaching and Learning

Only a small log building stood on the shores of St. Mary's Lake when Father Edward Sorin and seven Brothers of the Congregation of the Holy Cross came there in 1842 to establish a university. There were more faculty members than students. The first student was Alexis Coquillard, founder of South Bend. Although the early years were hard, the founders would be pleased to know that the institution they labored to create has become one of the best known in higher education—the University of Notre Dame du Lac, better known as Notre Dame.

The football teams, players, and coaches of Notre Dame have become legendary, particularly Knute Rockne, an alumnus of the school, who is considered by many to be the greatest football coach of all time. However, football is not permitted to overshadow the academic achievements of Notre Dame and the many graduates who gained fame in other fields.

Forerunner of Indiana University, Indiana Seminary opened in 1824 at Bloomington, but it did not become a college until 1828, and was called Indiana University ten years later. Today, many consider it to be one of the most notable of all state universities. An extraordinary number of its graduates have become presidents of other colleges. The count was seventy-five as early as 1941.

Indiana State University is at Terre Haute. It is one of the "big five" of Indiana's educational institutions. The others are Indiana University, Notre Dame, Ball State University, and Purdue.

The oldest continuously operating college in Indiana is Hanover College, Madison, founded as a Presbyterian college in 1827. Another college, Wabash, nicknamed Old Siwash, in Crawfordsville, was founded in 1832 and numbered Presbyterians among its founders. DePauw University, a Methodist institution, was founded in 1837 at Greencastle.

Distinguished Catholic colleges, in addition to Notre Dame, are St. Joseph's, Rensselaer; St. Mary's, South Bend; St. Francis, Fort Wayne; St. Mary-of-the-Woods, Terre Haute; St. Meinrad at St. Meinrad; and Marian at Indianapolis.

The largest Lutheran coeducational college in the United States is Valparaiso University, sometimes fondly called "the poor man's Harvard."

In 1869 John Purdue and other interested citizens of Lafayette contributed $200,000 to establish a university at Lafayette, and the name Purdue became one of the best known in higher education. Purdue is the "land grant" college of Indiana.

Butler University and Arthur Jordan Conservatory of Music are distinguished Indianapolis schools. Rose Polytechnic Institute is a leading scientific and technical institution, as is Ball State University, Muncie, in the field of education. Taylor University, Upland, and Goshen College, Goshen, are other Indiana institutions of higher learning.

Other Indiana colleges include Anderson College, Anderson; Earlham College, Richmond; Evansville College, Evansville; Indiana Central College, Indianapolis; Manchester College, North Manchester; Oakland City College, Oakland City; Tri-State College, Angola; and Indiana Institute of Technology, Fort Wayne.

Two of the nation's leading military schools are Culver and Howe.

Education in Indiana "came from the top down"; that is, there were adequate colleges before there was a general system of education in the lower grades. The 1816 constitution of Indiana was the first among all the states to call for a graduated system of schools from primary district schools through the university, open to all for free instruction. However, this was generally true only on paper until the 1852 free-school law became an important influence in the rapid growth of the public schools.

The contributions of New Harmony are often praised in educational histories. Its distinguished scholars and scientists gave much attention to education and created what has been called "a revolutionary educational center for the whole country."

Opposite: Combining culture and commerce
in University Park, Indianapolis.

The Soldiers and Sailors Monument, in the center of Monument Circle, is in downtown Indianapolis.

Enchantment of Indiana

"POLIS" OF INDIANA

The Greeks had a word for it, and that word has given Indiana's capital city its name. *Polis*, the Greek word for city, was combined with the name of the state, to come out "Indiana-polis." The capital city has a number of unique distinctions. It is said to be the largest city in the United States not located on navigable water, and its various memorials and monuments rank among the most expansive and imposing anywhere.

Soldiers and Sailors Monument, with its shaft soaring 284 feet (86.6 meters) into the sky, is thought to be the first major tribute of this kind to honor the enlisted serviceman. A worldwide contest was held to select a design for this monument, and the contest was won by a German architect, Bruno Schmitz. This dramatic shaft has been a well-loved feature of the capital since 1902; it is surrounded by terraced fountains and heroic sculptures.

Extending five square blocks, World War Memorial Plaza pays tribute to the men and women of Indiana who sacrificed their lives in the nation's cause during the two great wars. Dominating this impressive plaza is the Indiana World War Memorial and its Altar Room, devoted as a shrine to the American flag. Outside, the stupendous statue "Pro Patria" is said to be the largest bronze casting ever made in the United States. A 100-foot (30.5-meter) granite obelisk and a cenotaph are also outstanding features of Memorial Plaza. Singled out for special honor in the cenotaph is Indiana's James Bethel Gresham, one of the first three members of the American forces to lose his life during World War I. American Legion National Headquarters are also located in Memorial Plaza.

The imposing state capitol building was completed within original cost estimates. It may be the only such public building in the country for which it is possible to make that claim. Prominent features of the capitol are the grand halls—running the full length of the building on each floor—and the 234-foot (71.3-meter) dome. Southern prisoners of war contributed the bronze bust of Colonel Richard

Owen at the base of the dome on the main floor, in tribute to his kindness to them at Camp Morton. Four statues on the grounds recognize the work of Oliver P. Morton, Thomas A. Hendricks, Robert Dale Owen, and Christopher Columbus. In the basement of the statehouse is the state museum.

Points of interest in Indianapolis include Crown Hill Cemetery, the great Scottish Rite Cathedral, Fort Benjamin Harrison, the Benjamin Harrison house, and the homes of writers James Whitcomb Riley and Booth Tarkington. The Indianapolis central library is a masterpiece of architecture. The Indiana State Library and Historical Building is often described as "the state of Indiana's most beautiful building."

Two worthwhile Indianapolis museums are the Children's Museum, with thirty rooms and twenty-five thousand items of particular interest to young people, and the John Herron Art Institute. Clowes Hall, an architectural wonder and home of the Indianapolis Symphony and other art, music, and dramatic activities, is on the Butler University campus.

Every year Indianapolis is host at Speedway City to the internationally renowned 500-mile (805-kilometers) race, where some of the fastest cars in the world burn up the speedway.

THE NORTHWEST

West of Indianapolis is Danville, with its interesting story of how its people "kidnapped" Central Normal College. In 1878 the college was at Ladoga, which had difficulty in housing all the students. At four o'clock one morning a half-mile-long (.8 kilometer) procession of wagons and buggies made off with almost all the moveable property of the college, plus the whole student body, and relocated it permanently in Danville.

The Boone County Courthouse at Lebanon is supported by the largest hand-hewn limestone pillars ever cut. The Lew Wallace Study at Crawfordsville is a strangely ornate building in Turkish style, in tribute to its owner's diplomatic assignment in Turkey. A

Shades State Park preserves some of the most beautiful virgin timberland in the state.

few miles south and west is some of the most beautiful virgin timberland in Indiana, preserved in Turkey Run and in Shades state parks.

The memorial bridge across the Wabash River at Attica is dedicated to Paul Dresser, who helped to make that river famous with "On the Banks of the Wabash," now the official song of the state. The great Dan Patch, the world's great harness-pacing horse, is still remembered in the Oxford country where he was stabled.

The most notable institution of Lafayette is Purdue, with its 6,107-seat Elliott Hall of Music. This is one of the largest theaters in the world. To honor the great French friend of America for whom the city is named, there is a statue of Lafayette by noted sculptor Lorado Taft. Those who commissioned this statue were among the first to recognize the genius of the sculptor, who later received much acclaim. Taft later recalled: "The LaFayette [statue] was about the first order I had in Chicago as I arrived there with high hopes—and little else—the first day of 1886. It was a copy of Bartholdi's 'LaFayette' in New York City that was required of me and one tiny photograph of that figure was all that was given me for data. I wonder at the temerity of youth, but I had to have the money and that supplies unlimited courage."

The restoration of Fort Ouiatenon near Lafayette.

Near Lafayette is the restoration of Fort Ouiatenon, originally built in 1717, one of the three French forts in Indiana.

August 17, 1859, a balloon carrying 123 letters of U.S. postage arose from Lafayette on what was supposed to be a flight to New York. The balloon and cargo came down 27 miles (43.4 kilometers) away, and the mail went the rest of the way by train. Many claims are made to the first airmail flight in history, but this may well be the earliest.

North of Lafayette is Tippecanoe Battlefield State Memorial, on the site of the battle. The Tippecanoe Historical Museum in Lafayette preserves many relics recovered from the battlefield.

Marquette Park in Gary is one of the finest city parks in the Midwest. Gary is the largest U.S. city founded in the twentieth century. To the east are the famed Indiana dunes. The former Indiana Dunes State Park, popular for recreation and nature study, became the major section of the new Indiana Dunes National Lakeshore.

Michigan City has an International Friendship Gardens. The theme of friendship is carried out by gifts of plants and shrubs to the gardens from hundreds of well-known leaders all over the world. For a city of its size, Michigan City's zoo is particularly outstanding, as is its annual Summer Festival. South Bend has a four-hundred-year-old tree, the Council Oak. It was here that La Salle and the Indians came to their historic agreement. Northern Indiana Historical Society Museum and Pierre Navarre Cabin, the trading post of South Bend's first settler, also are of interest.

The campus of the University of Notre Dame, comprising 1,700 acres (688 hectares), is one of the largest in the world. The many art treasures of the university attract many visitors. In the library are paintings of Tintoretto, Veronese, Bartolomeo, Murillo, Van Dyck, and many others. The collection of furniture of the Medici and Borgia families and other art objects is outstanding. A former art department head at Notre Dame, Luigi Gregory, created many of the noted murals in the university buildings.

There is an impressive monument where the village of Chief Menominee once stood, near Plymouth.

THE NORTHEAST

"Elkhart" is supposed to come from the Indians, who said an island in the St. Joseph River was shaped like the heart of an elk. Famed evangelist Billy Sunday built his tabernacle at Winona Lake, near Warsaw, a huge building seating 7,500 people. Wabash claims to be the first electrically lighted city in the United States. In its courthouse square stands the 35-ton (31.5-metric ton) statue of Abraham Lincoln, "Lincoln of the People," cast in bronze. Miami County Historical Museums, Peru, owns more than forty thousand items, including many from pioneer times. The Frances Slocum Trail from Peru makes a fascinating tour, combining history, nostalgia, and scenery, along the Seven Pillars cliff formation.

Kokomo recognizes the accomplishments of Elwood Haynes, father of the modern automobile, with the Haynes Memorial, erected where his first car was successfully tested. Highland Park, at Kokomo, has several unique landmarks, including Old Ben, a stuffed steer said to be one of the largest.

Much of northeast Indiana is Gene Stratton Porter country. The large log house, occupied by Mrs. Porter for many years, has been preserved as a memorial to her in Limberlost State Memorial, near Geneva. (The region took its unusual name from "Limber Jim" Corbus, who was said to have been "lost" in swamp quicksand.) In 1913, considering the Limberlost region too developed, Mrs. Porter built a new home in Wildflower Woods near Rome City. This has been preserved as Gene Stratton Porter State Memorial.

In Swinney Park at Fort Wayne is the combined city and county Historical Museum. Johnny Appleseed Memorial Park honors the man who is buried there. The Lincoln Museum at Fort Wayne is said to have the largest collection of literature ever assembled on Abraham Lincoln. The historic city seems to evoke the long-gone sounds of the Indians of Miami Town, the cries of prisoners tortured there by the Indians, and the massacre of 1813.

Huntington is noted for its unusual bridge. One side of the bridge is lined with stores and shops for its entire length.

At Anderson, the Church of God maintains its international headquarters. In nearby Mounds State Park is the largest prehistoric earthworks in Indiana: an earthen wall 9 feet (2.7 meters) high and a quarter of a mile (.4 kilometer) long. Muncie takes its name from the Munsee tribe of Delaware Indians. Its Ball State University has a notable art building, housing paintings of Rembrandt, Raphael,

Circus City Festival, Peru.

Titian, Renoir, Degas, and others—gifts of the Ball brothers. Greenfield is the birthplace of James Whitcomb Riley and the site of his Old Swimmin' Hole. Richmond's statue of Riley was made possible through contributions of children's pennies. New Castle has erected a monument to its native son—Wilbur Wright, airplane co-inventor.

At Richmond is the Madonna of the Trails statue, one of twelve along Highway 40, erected to honor pioneer women. In Richmond, Henry Clay was publicly challenged to free his fifty slaves when he made a speech before twenty thousand people. His angry reply drew national attention and may have helped to defeat him in the contest with Polk.

The lake region of northeast Indiana is a popular summer resort area. Winter sports are enjoyed at Pokagon State Park and at Mt. Wawasee, near New Paris.

THE SOUTHEAST

Connersville is the site of Mary Gray Bird Sanctuary. The grave of Wendell Willkie, and a memorial to him, are at Rushville. Greensburg is noted for a tree that grows out of the courthouse tower. West Harrison has a split personality: half of its Main street is in Indiana, the other half in Ohio. Lawrenceburg is where Henry Ward Beecher had his first pastorate, and Beecher Presbyterian Church is where the noted preacher and orator spent two and a half years. At Metamora, a section of the Whitewater Canal has been restored, including an aqueduct and lock. A power launch operates there in season.

The wine that once made the Swiss colony of Vevay famous is no longer produced there. One of the winemakers left a will in which he directed that no more than $2 be spent for his funeral, and his mourners were instructed to drink his large supply of ale and wine before he was buried.

Until 1830, Madison was the largest town in Indiana. It is renowned for its many fine buildings of classical architecture. Best known of these is the beautiful home of James D. Lanier, who helped Indiana finance her Civil War effort. One of the finest in the Ohio Valley, the home is maintained as a state memorial, and visitors marvel particularly at the three-story, unsupported spiral staircase. Other fine buildings are being restored in the community by Historic Madison, Inc. Madison is home of the Madison Regatta, a powerboat race of national prominence.

The railroad, on entering Madison, ascends the steepest slope of any in the world (not using cogs or cables). Near Madison is beautiful Clifty Falls.

Jeffersonville was built according to plans by Thomas Jefferson. It is the site of the first penitentiary in Indiana, and was leased to private operators who kept the prisoners on a commercial basis. Near Jeffersonville, Henry Clay and Humphrey Marshall fought a famous duel in which both received flesh wounds. Also at Jeffersonville is the Howard National Steamboat Museum, at Howard Shipyards, where many famous nineteenth-century boats were built.

The old state capitol building at Corydon is maintained as a memorial to the one-time luster of the small community.

A COLORFUL COUNTY NAMED BROWN

Brown County is renowned for scenery and tourist attractions. Some communities in Brown County have unique, imaginative names: Bean Blossom, Needmore, and Gnaw Bone. Gnaw Bone claims its name was born when one local man asked another where a third one was. The answer: "I seed him settin' on a log above the sawmill a'gnawing on a bone." The state tried to get the name changed, but without success.

One of the most unique monuments is Poplar Tree monument at Gnaw Bone. John Allcorn was sawing down a poplar tree when it fell and crushed him to death, and wood from that tree was used for his casket. After he was buried, the wood of the casket sprouted and a tree grew, which is now his memorial.

Nashville, in Brown County, is the home of many artists, writers, and craftsmen. Among its noted crafts are weaving and doll making.

This is one of the more than thirty covered bridges in Parke County, which has an annual Covered Bridge Festival in October.

Liars' Bench, in front of the courthouse at Nashville, seats six and has an arm on only one end. When someone who is standing tells a better story than those who are seated, the one on the end is pushed off to make room for the winner.

Brown County State Park, near Nashville, covers more than 15,000 acres (6,070 hectares) of beautiful country. It is the largest state park in Indiana. T.C. Steele State Memorial, at Belmont, honors the renowned artist who gave Brown County its reputation as an art center. Trailside Museum features a number of his best works.

Nearby is Columbus, renowned for its architecture.

THE HISTORIC SOUTHWEST

Martinsville is the home of the world's largest goldfish hatchery. McCormick's Creek State Park was the first Indiana state park.

Notable features of Indiana University at Bloomington are the Lilly Library, featuring rare books, the Lincoln Library, and the

Dailey collection of art. One of the best-known American artists, Thomas Hart Benton, created the university auditorium's murals.

A ghost village, built about 1816, has been restored in Spring Mill State Park near Mitchell. It has a cobbler shop, boot house, pottery plant, gristmill with water wheel, still house, apothecary, tavern, and homes of pioneers.

Silver Treasure Cave of McBridges Bluffs near Dover Hill excites treasure seekers. Bars of buried silver treasure have been found there, but the main part of the treasure has never been located. Other unusual caves of the area are River Cave, where visitors take "the world's longest underground boat ride;" Marengo Cave; and Wyandotte Cave, said to be one of the largest on the continent. Inside Wyandotte Cave is the world's highest underground hill—175 feet (53.3 meters) tall—called Monument Mountain.

Tell City was laid out by its ambitious Swiss founders to be a city of ninety thousand people. It has not yet reached that size.

The region of southern Indiana where Lincoln grew to manhood is called Lincoln Land. Here is the Lincoln Boyhood National Memorial. The showplace of Rockport is Lincoln Pioneer Village. Here, reconstructed, are homes of Indiana people who

Hamer's Mill, in Spring Mill State Park near Mitchell.

The Ohio River's Horseshoe Bend.

played a prominent part in Lincoln's life. In memory of Lincoln's mother, Nancy Hanks Lincoln Memorial stands near where she died, in what is called Lincoln City. The memorial is noted for its sculptured panels.

St. Meinrad Abbey, built in 1852 of native stone, is well known for its choir and elaborate altars.

Another southern Indiana community has gained international fame because of its name. The settlers wanted to call it Santa Fe, but there was already a Santa Fe in Indiana; so they named it Santa Claus because it was Christmas. Every year thousands of children enjoy the children's features there, and hundreds of thousands of pieces of mail flood in at Christmas time.

Evansville has a fine symphony orchestra, the Evansville Philharmonic. It gained international fame when renowned composer-conductor George Dasch was engaged as its musical director.

Near Evansville is Angel Mounds, where many valuable prehistoric finds have been made. In the area where the Wabash joins the Ohio River is Hovey Lake, where cypress, pelicans, and other fauna and flora not found elsewhere in Indiana may be seen.

Some of the communities on the Wabash River are among the most historic in Indiana.

Fort Harrison, 3 miles (4.8 kilometers) north of Terre Haute, was built by William Henry Harrison and later defended by Zachary Taylor, both of whom became presidents of the United States. Eugene Debs was born in Terre Haute, and there he founded the first industrial union in America, the American Railway Union. Swope Art Gallery features the work of ousstandi g artists. Wheels Museum, at Terre Haute, has a fine collection of old cars.

The oldest town in Indiana is Vincennes, named for its founder, François de Vincennes. During its early French days, Vincennes was a joyful and colorful place. Masquerades, balls, singing, folk tales, and other simple pleasures were enjoyed by the French people. Today's annual Creole Ball has its inspiration in this period. The old French cemetery at Vincennes is most interesting.

In five years, beginning in 1834, when beloved Bishop Gabriel Bruté served at Vincennes, he organized a flourishing Catholic organization throughout Indiana.

Splendid St. Francis Xavier Cathedral, which dominates Vincennes, was begun in 1825. In its tower is a bell recast from the "Little Liberty Bell." This bell was rung in the original log chapel, calling the people together to sign the oath of allegiance to the Americans under George Rogers Clark at the urging of Father Gibault. The cathedral library has an invaluable collection of rare books and old records.

The Old Cathedral, Vincennes.

The magnificent State Memorial to George Rogers Clark at Vincennes was dedicated in 1936 by President Franklin D. Roosevelt.

Among the Vincennes structures that have been preserved or restored for visitors are the William Henry Harrison home, the Zachary Taylor home, and the first newspaper print shop in Indiana. Harrison's home, Grouseland, has been refurnished as a historic shrine.

The Lincoln Memorial Bridge spans the Wabash at Vincennes, where the Lincoln family left Indiana for Illinois. For those interested in archaeology, there is 140-foot-high (42.7 meters) Sugar Loaf Mound, a burial place near Vincennes used by prehistoric peoples.

At New Harmony are reminders of the two attempts to set up a perfect society. The Barrett-Gate House incorporates part of the first building built at New Harmony. The dye house was one of the first plants of this kind west of the Appalachian Mountains. In its two-story drying well long strands of newly dyed yarn would hang so that their weight would keep them from shrinking. The library of Workingmen's Institute, Rapp-Maclure Mansion, and the laboratory of Dr. David Dale Owen are historic structures that are still to be seen at New Harmony.

An extraordinary, modern New Harmony building is the "Roofless Church," built to illustrate the belief that "only one roof—the sky—is vast enough to embrace all worshipping humanity." Its shape resembles a billowing parachute settling to earth, and it features an extraordinary statue, "Descent of the Holy Spirit," by sculptor Jacques Lipchitz.

On Gabriel's Rock at New Harmony are the imprints of two human feet. Members of the Rappite sect who founded Harmonie believed these to be the imprint of the Angel Gabriel, bringing messages to Father Rapp, their leader. It has never been determined whether these footprints are prehistoric or simply a clever sculpture.

The hopes of Father Rapp and Robert Owen were never fully realized at New Harmony, but similar desires for a better life inspire their heirs, the people of Indiana, who strive to preserve and extend the blessings of their state and their nation.

Handy Reference Section

Instant Facts

Became the 19th state, December 11, 1816
Capital—Indianapolis, founded 1821
Nickname—The Hoosier State
Motto—"Crossroads of America"
State bird—Cardinal
State tree—Tulip poplar
State flower—Peony (*paeonia*)
State stone—Limestone
State Song—"On the Banks of the Wabash," by Paul Dresser
Area—36,291 square miles (93,993 square kilometers)
Rank in area—38th
Greatest length (north to south)—276 miles (444 kilometers)
Greatest width (east to west)—177 miles (285 kilometers)
Geographic center—Boone
Highest point—1,285 feet (391.67 meters), Randolph County
Lowest point—313 feet (95.4 meters), Vanderburgh County
Number of counties—92
Population—5,782,000 (1980 projection)
Rank in population—11th
Population density—159.3 per square mile (61.5 per square kilometer),
                          1980 projection
Rank in density—13th
Population center—Clinton County, 13.8 miles (22.2 kilometers) southeast
                          of Frankfort
Birthrate—15.8 per 1,000
Infant mortality rate—17.8 per 1,000
Physicians per 100,000—105

Principal cities—		
Indianapolis	746,302	(1970 census)
Fort Wayne	178,021	
Gary	175,415	
Evansville	138,764	
South Bend	125,580	
Hammond	107,885	

You Have A Date with History

1679—Robert Cavalier, Sieur de LaSalle, visits Indiana
1732-33—François Morgane de Vincennes founds Vincennes
1763—French give up hold on region
1777—British troops occupy Indiana

1779—George Rogers Clark recaptures Vincennes
1784—Virginia gives up claim to Indiana
1787—Indiana becomes part of Northwest Territory
1794—Anthony Wayne establishes Fort Wayne
1800—Indiana Territory created
1809—Indiana Territory established within present boundaries
1811—Indians defeated at Battle of Tippecanoe
1813—Capital moved to Corydon
1816—Statehood
1825—Indianapolis becomes state capital
1832—Wabash and Erie Canal begun
1836—Internal Improvement Bill passed
1842—University of Notre Dame opened
1851—New state constitution
1860—Indiana Republicans help elect Lincoln
1861—Governor Morton responds to Lincoln's appeal for soldiers
1863—Confederate General Morgan invades Indiana
1865—Martyred Abraham Lincoln lies in state at Indianapolis
1868—James Oliver perfects chilled-steel plow
1887—State capitol finished
1894—Elwood Haynes perfects first "modern" automobile
1905—Gary founded
1911—First 500-mile race at Indianapolis
1918—130,670 from Indiana serve in World War I
1937—Disastrous Ohio Valley flood
1940—Wendell Willkie defeated for presidency
1946—338,000 Indianans serve in World War II
1965—Bills introduced in Congress to create Burns Ditch port and national dunes park
1966—Indiana celebrates 150th anniversary of statehood
1970—Under Unigov plan, Indianapolis expands over 300 square miles, covering most of Marion County
1970—Port of Indiana opens on Lake Michigan
1976—Indiana Dunes National Lake Shore expanded

Thinkers, Doers, Fighters
People of renown who have been associated with Indiana

Ade, George
Beard, Charles Austin
Beard, Mary
Beveridge, Albert J.
Bruté, Gabriel
Burnside, Ambrose E.

Carmichael, Hoagland (Hoagy)
Cavalier, Robert, Sieur de La Salle
Chapman, Jonathan (Johnny Appleseed)
Clark, George Rogers
Coffin, Levi
Colfax, Schuyler

89

Dasch, George
Dreiser, Theodore
Dresser, Paul
Eggleston, Edward
Evans, John
Fauntleroy, Constance
Gary, Elbert H.
Hammond, George H.
Harrison, Benjamin
Harrison, William Henry
Hay, John
Haynes, Elwood
Lanier, James D.
Lincoln, Abraham
Maclure, William
Marshall, Thomas R.
Morton, Oliver P.
Oliver, James
Owen, Robert

Owen, Robert Dale
Owen, David Dale
Porter, Cole
Purdue, John
Pyle, Ernie
Riley, James Whitcomb
Smith, Caleb B.
Steele, Theodore Clement
Studebaker, Clement
Studebaker, Henry
Sunday, William Ashley (Billy)
Tarkington, Booth
Taylor, Zachary
*Wallace, Lew
Wayne, Anthony
Westendorf, Thomas Paine
Willkie, Wendell Lewis
Winter, George
Wright, Wilbur

*Indiana's representative in the national Statuary Hall

Governors of the State of Indiana

Jonathan Jennings 1816-22
Ratliff Boon 1822
William Hendricks 1822-25
James Brown Ray 1825-31
Noah Noble 1831-37
David Wallace 1837-40
Samuel Bigger 1840-43
James Whitcomb 1843-48
Paris C. Dunning 1848-49
Joseph A. Wright 1849-57
Ashbel P. Willard 1857-60
Abram A. Hammond 1860-61
Henry S. Lane 1861
Oliver P. Morton 1861-67
Conrad Baker 1867-73
Thomas A. Hendricks 1873-77
James D. Williams 1877-80
Isaac P. Gray 1880-81
Albert G. Porter 1881-85
Alvin P. Hovey 1889-91
Ira J. Chase 1891-93
Claude Matthews 1893-97

James A. Mount 1897-1901
Winfield T. Durbin 1901-05
J. Frank Hanly 1905-09
Thomas R. Marshall 1909-13
Samuel M. Ralston 1913-17
James P. Goodrich 1917-21
Warren T. McCray 1921-24
Emmet F. Branch 1924-25
Ed Jackson 1925-29
Harry G. Leslie 1929-33
Paul V. McNutt 1933-37
M. Clifford Townsend 1937-41
Henry F. Schricker 1941-45
Ralph F. Gates 1945-49
Henry F. Schricker 1949-53
George Craig 1953-57
Harold W. Handley 1957-61
Matthew E. Welsh 1961-65
Roger D. Branigin 1965-69
Edgar D. Whitcomb 1969-73
Otis R. Bowen 1973-

Index

92

95

PICTURE CREDITS

Color photographs courtesy of the following: Jim Rowan, Cover; Richard Cunningham, 2-3; Department of Commerce, State of Indiana, 8, 12, 34, 43, 44, 46, 48, 51, 52, 56, 73, 77, 78, 80, 83; USDI, NPS, Indiana Dunes National Lakeshore, 14; USDI, NPS, George Rogers Clark Memorial National Historical Park, 23; U.S. Army, 26; White House Collection, 37; Hooks Drug Stores, James M. Rogers, 40, 41; U.S. Steel Corporation, 47; Indianapolis Museum of Art, 61.

Illustrations on back cover by Len W. Meents.

ABOUT THE AUTHOR

With the publication of his first book for school use when he was twenty, **Allan Carpenter** began a career as an author that has spanned more than 135 books. After teaching in the public schools of Des Moines, Mr. Carpenter began his career as an educational publisher at the age of twenty-one when he founded the magazine *Teachers Digest.* In the field of educational periodicals, he was responsible for many innovations. During his many years in publishing, he has perfected a highly organized approach to handling large volumes of factual material: after extensive traveling and having collected all possible materials, he systematically reviews and organizes everything. From his apartment high in Chicago's John Hancock Building, Allan recalls, "My collection and assimilation of materials on the states and countries began before the publication of my first book." Allan is the founder of Carpenter Publishing House and of Infordata International, Inc., publishers of *Issues in Education* and *Index to U. S. Government Periodicals.* When he is not writing or traveling, his principal avocation is music. He has been the principal bassist of many symphonies, and he managed the country's leading non-professional symphony for twenty-five years.